GNVQ Core Skills

COMMUNICATION

Intermediate/Advanced

GNVQ Core Skills

COMMUNICATION

Intermediate/Advanced

William Melrose

**Lecturer in Management Studies
at Halton College**

PITMAN PUBLISHING
128 Long Acre, London WC2E 9AN

A Division of Longman Group Limited

First published in 1994

© William Melrose 1994

A CIP catalogue record for this book can be obtained from the British Library.

ISBN 0 273 60627 1

10 9 8 7 6 5 4 3

Typeset by M Rules.
Printed and bound in Great Britain by Clays Ltd, St Ives plc

The Publishers' policy is to use paper manufactured from sustainable forests.

Contents

To Judith and Joy

Acknowledgements

My thanks go to my wife Judith for her support while I was writing this book and for her invaluable help with the word processing difficulties which I got into and from which she managed to extricate me.

I should also like to thank the technical staff of the Learning Resources Centre at Halton College and Ann Sharrock of Manchester University Computer Centre who gave me a great deal of technical help and advice.

I am also grateful to Gordon Riach of Edinburgh for the artwork and Anthony's Travel of Runcorn for the use of their letterhead.

Introduction

The aim of this book is to cover the skills and knowledge which are required to deal with the range of situations suggested by the National Council for Vocational Qualifications for GNVQ Communication, levels 2 and 3 (intermediate and advanced). This aim will be achieved by means of two approaches.

The first uses a number of worked examples from which students will be able to learn the principles covered by the element being studied. These worked examples are called 'tasks'; suggested solutions to the tasks appear at the end of the book, where appropriate.

With the second approach, the book covers the background knowledge and thus reinforces the principles covered by the tasks from a theoretical point of view. Every effort has been made to demonstrate clearly the link between the principles in the tasks and the supporting background information.

Each chapter in the book represents one of the four elements of the Core Skills Units in Communication for both levels 2 and 3, with tasks of varying degrees of difficulty to suit students at level 2 or 3. Each task is given a number which corresponds to the suggested solution of the same number at the end of the book. As well as the task number, there will be a code number in brackets to indicate the level: (L2) for level 2, (L3) for level 3. The codes are there for guidance only, and it is up to tutors to decide on the ability of each group. The guiding principle should not be the code numbers, but how well the students manage to grasp the principles incorporated in the tasks. At the beginning of each chapter there is also a statement of the objectives that students are expected to achieve if they are to pass the element.

Following is the standard checklist which you might find useful for keeping track of the areas which have to be covered in each element.

COMMUNICATION LEVEL 2

Element 2.1: Take part in discussions with a range of people on routine matters

Performance criteria:

1 own contributions are clear and appropriate to the subject matter

2 own contributions are made in a tone and manner suited to the audience

3 contributions from others are listened to attentively

4 own understanding of points made by others is actively checked and confirmed

Range: **Subject matters:** routine matters (eg. responding to day-to-day enquiries; discussing routine tasks)

Mode: face to face; using the telephone

Audience: people familiar with the subject matter and in frequent contact with the individual (eg. supervisors, colleagues, peers, tutors); people familiar with the subject matter but not in frequent contact with the individual (eg. some customers/clients)

Element 2.2: Prepare written material on routine matters

Performance criteria:

1 all necessary information is included and information is accurate

2 documents are legible

3 grammar and punctuation follow standard conventions, and words used routinely are spelled correctly

4 the format used is appropriate to the nature of the material and information is ordered appropriately to maximize audience understanding

Range: **Subject matters:** routine matters (eg. day-to-day organization and administration; responding to customers' letters)

Format: pre-set formats (eg. record and report cards, memos); outline formats (eg. letters, reports, log book entries)

Conventions: use of full stop, comma, apostrophe, capital letters, sentences and paragraphs

Audience: people familiar with the subject matter and in frequent contact with the individual (eg. supervisors, colleagues, peers, tutors);

people familiar with the subject matter but not in frequent contact with the individual (eg. some customers/clients)

Element 2.3: Use images to illustrate points made in writing and in discussions with a range of people on routine matters

Performance criteria:

1   images are used to support main points in the communication

2   images provide clear illustration of the point(s) to which they refer

3   the points at which images are used are appropriate

Range: **Subject matters:** routine matters (eg. day-to-day organization and administration; responding to customers' letters)

Images: selected from those readily available in the context; produced to meet a specific need (eg. sketches, diagrams, still photographs, charts)

Audience: people familiar with the subject matter and in frequent contact with the individual (eg. supervisors, colleagues, peers, tutors); people familiar with the subject matter but not in frequent contact with the individual (eg. some customers/clients)

Element 2.4: Read and respond to written material and images on routine matters

Performance criteria:

1   main points are accurately identified

2   the meaning of unfamiliar words, phrases and images is accurately identified using the sources provided

Range: **Subject matters:** routine matters (eg. day-to-day organization and administration; responding to customers' letters)

Format: pre-set formats (eg. record and report cards, memos); outline formats (eg. letters, reports, log book entries)

Images: used commonly in the context (eg. sketches, diagrams, still photographs, charts)

Sources of clarification: provided for the individual: written (eg. dictionaries, manuals); oral (eg. supervisors, tutors, colleagues)

COMMUNICATION LEVEL 3

Element 3.1: Take part in discussions with a range of people on a range of matters

Performance criteria:

1 own contributions are expressed effectively for their purpose and are appropriate to the subject matter

2 own contributions are made in a tone and manner suited to the audience

3 others are explicitly encouraged to contribute and their contributions listened to attentively

4 own understanding of points made by others is actively checked and confirmed

Range: **Subject matters:** routine matters (eg. responding to day-to-day enquiries; discussing routine tasks); complex and non-routine matters (eg. solving problems, dealing with sensitive issues)

Mode: face to face; using the telephone

Audience: people familiar with the subject matter and in frequent contact with the individual (eg. supervisors, colleagues, peers, tutors); people familiar with the subject matter but not in frequent contact with the individual (eg. some customers/clients); people unfamiliar with the subject matter and not in frequent contact with the individual (eg. some customers/clients, visitors)

Element 3.2: Prepare written material on a range of matters

Performance criteria:

1 the fullness and accuracy of information included is appropriate to the purpose and needs of the audience

2 documents are legible

3 grammar, punctuation and spelling follow standard conventions

4 the format used is appropriate to the purpose of the material and information is ordered appropriately to maximize audience understanding

Range: **Subject matters:** routine matters (eg. day-to-day organization and administration; handling customers' letters); complex and non-routine matters (eg. a report on a piece of research; a letter on a sensitive issue; summarizing a complex document)

Format: pre-set formats (eg. record and report cards, memos); outline formats (eg. letters, reports, log book entries); freely structured documents (where the structure is determined by the individual)

Conventions: use of full stop, comma, apostrophe, colon, semi-colon, capital letters, sentences, paragraphs; use of highlighting and indentation to enhance meaning

Audience: people familiar with the subject matter and in frequent contact with the individual (eg. supervisors, colleagues, peers, tutors); people familiar with the subject matter but not in frequent contact with the individual (eg. some customers/clients); people unfamiliar with the subject matter and not in frequent contact with the individual (eg. some customers/clients, visitors)

Element 3.3: Use images to illustrate points made in writing and in discussions with a range of people on a range of matters

Performance criteria:

1   images are used to support main points and others which the audience may have difficulty understanding

2   images provide clear illustration of the point(s) to which they refer

3   the points at which images are used are appropriate

Range: **Subject matters:** routine matters (eg. day-to-day organization and administration; handling customers' letters); complex and non-routine matters (eg. a report on a piece of research; a letter on a sensitive issue)

Images: selected from those readily available in the context; produced to meet a specific need (eg. sketches, diagrams, still photographs, charts)

Audience: people familiar with the subject matter and in frequent contact with the individual (eg. supervisors, colleagues, peers, tutors); people familiar with the subject matter but not in frequent contact with the individual (eg. some customers/clients); people unfamiliar with the subject matter and not in frequent contact with the individual (eg. some customers/clients, visitors)

Element 3.4 Read and respond to written material and images on a range of matters

Performance criteria:

1   main points are accurately identified

2   the meaning of unfamiliar words, phrases and images is accurately identified

3   appropriate sources of clarification are used

Range: **Subject matters:** routine matters (eg. day-to-day organization and administration; handling customers' letters); complex and non-routine matters (eg. a report on a piece of research; a letter on a sensitive issue)

Format: pre-set formats (eg. record and report cards, memos); outline formats (eg. letters, reports, log book entries); freely structured (eg. wide variety of documents from publicity materials to books and formal reports)

Images: used commonly in the context (eg. sketches, diagrams, still photographs, charts); images which have been used by others to illustrate complex/difficult points

Sources of clarification: provided for the individual; having to be identified and sought out by the individual: written (eg. dictionaries, manuals); oral (eg. supervisors, tutors, colleagues)

1

Speaking to people

This chapter covers Elements 2.1 and 3.1

The overall aim of the Elements 2.1 and 3.1 is to ensure that students can take part in discussions with a range of people on a wide variety of subjects.

OBJECTIVES

At the end of the elements students will be able to make contributions to discussions with a range of people about both routine and complex matters:

1 presenting information which is clear and appropriate to the subject matter;

2 expressing themselves effectively for their purpose;

3 using a tone and a manner which are appropriate to the audience;

4 listening attentively to the contributions of others;

5 while explicitly encouraging others to make their contributions.

All of the above objectives will be achieved, either in a face to face situation, or on the telephone.

How should we speak?

Speaking to people is probably the most common way of communicating with others. We do it naturally, and without thinking too much beforehand, and this is where the problems usually begin. People tend to get into the habit of speaking in a certain way, and of using certain words and phrases regardless of the situation.

We should be aware that both the situation in which we find ourselves having to speak and the audience to whom we are speaking should have an influence on how we speak.

Be aware of whom you are speaking to

Most of the time we are not in control of this process because we cope with different situations by responding in our own individual natural ways, assuming that, if we ourselves know what we mean, everything will be all right. Our experiences in life should tell us how wrong that assumption often is. The way we talk to others is the result of a variety of environmental influences, such as the kind of school we went to, the way we were treated at school, whether we were a success there or not, our home life, the community we grew up in and so on.

Speaking to someone we know well and who knows us well is easy. Normally this means that we can be 'ourselves', that we do not feel the need to put on any kind of act in order to influence the way others see us. Because the other person knows us, we expect him or her to have already formed an opinion about us.

When we come across a new situation in life, however, we cannot expect to be able to speak to people in the way we have been used to. In this situation we have to put greater thought into how we speak. This means paying attention to:

- the kind of words we choose;
- the tone of voice we use;
- the message we mean to get across to our audience.

A good illustration of this is when we are starting a new job.

If you are lucky enough to join the ranks of the employed for the first time, you will find yourself in an entirely new world, especially if you have just come from school or college.

There will be many things which are unfamiliar to you and you will have a large number of questions to ask in order to clear up any gaps in your understanding. You must try to avoid assuming certain things which might irritate other people. An example of this is shown in Task 1.

 ## TASK 1 (L2)

You have arrived at your new place of employment and have been told by reception to go to the Accounts Department and ask for Mrs Jennings. After trying to follow the directions you have been given, you get lost and are not sure where you are or how to get to the Accounts Department. You decide to ask a tall man in a dark suit for help and say to him:

'Excuse me, mate, tell us how to get to the Accounts Department, will yer?'

He looks at you for a few seconds and says, somewhat surprisingly:

'No, I can't. Ask someone else.'

Think of as many reasons as you can why the man answered you in the way he did. Discuss your answers with the others in your group before checking them with the suggested solutions at the end of the book.

You must get used to the *hierarchy of authority*. Whether you have come from school, college or another employer, this new place of work will have an authority structure which is different from what you have been used to. It is up to you to familiarize yourself with who has what degree of authority. People who have joined the firm with a high level of professional expertise will be rewarded with a corresponding level of respect as a consequence of their qualifications and experience, but for those who join as school or college leavers, status will be fairly low.

TASK 2 (L2)

Assume you are in the same situation as the one in Task 1, and ask the same man the question in a way which is more likely to produce a favourable response. It is a good idea for you to role play this in front of the other members of the group and invite their comments.

It is clear, therefore, that when you are talking to people in general or asking them specific questions, you have to consider your situation carefully and take into account your relationship with the person or persons to whom you are speaking. You have to think carefully about how you are going to approach this so that people will be clear about what you mean, and so that you will be given the correct information. You should always take care not only regarding what you say but also when and where you say it. Special care is needed in the following situations:

- when you are speaking to someone of a different status;
- when you are speaking to someone of the opposite sex;
- when you are speaking to someone you have not met before. (This is particularly important if you are representing your company.)

Status differences

There is usually some difference in status between two people who are talking to each other. The only time that status differences are not important is when we are with groups of friends, and even then someone sometimes becomes 'top dog' in the group, almost like a leader.

The difference in the status between individuals, or between individuals and groups, means that what they say and how they say it tend to have marked variations. Such differences in the way people speak have a knock-on effect. For example, someone in authority could become too authoritarian, almost like a dictator. On the other hand, someone who is in a subordinate position could become subservient.

Someone in authority could become too authoritarian

You should strive to be able to say what you feel and believe, without putting other people down because of your views or feelings. In other words, you should be assertive. You should avoid:

- allowing assertiveness to become aggressiveness, and
- allowing your assertiveness to be undermined so that your real feelings and opinions are not being communicated.

TASK 3 (L2)

Imagine that you are a part-time shelf filler in a large supermarket like Tesco's or Sainsbury's, and you have often thought that it might be a good idea to have a place set aside for parents to leave their children while they do their shopping. One day, the area manager, Mr Wilson, is in the store and you want to tell him about your idea. After all, it could mean that you will be offered a full-time job if he likes the idea.

Write down how you would approach him and what you would say to introduce your idea. Practise what you would say by yourself before trying it out in front of the group with another person role playing the area manager. It has to be said that it is unusual for a part-time shelf filler to attempt this but if you are keen to have a full-time job then a desperate remedy is sometimes a short-cut to achieving your goal. (See suggested solution.)

No matter how good we are at our job there is usually one task which we always have difficulty with and this can get us into trouble with our superiors. Bear this in mind when you attempt the next task.

TASK 4 (L3)

You have been working as a clerical trainee in a busy builders' merchant's office and part of your duties involves doing the petty cash account summary every Friday morning so that your manager can have it for the Friday afternoon meeting with the Managing Director. Because he likes the information by 11 am every Friday, the account runs from Friday to Thursday. Although you do not find accounting work very difficult, somehow this task always takes you about twice the time that you have been allocated to do it. It is possibly because there seems to be a large number of items to be entered, which is very time consuming, and then it is always difficult to balance the petty cash because people take the wrong amount, or forget to fill in a petty cash voucher for what they have taken. The result is that your manager seldom has the petty cash account before 12 noon, and often it is later than that.

Understandably, your manager Mrs Thompson is annoyed by this and calls you into her office one Monday to talk to you about it. Her opening remarks might be:

> 'Jane (or James), it's your job to let me have the petty cash account by 11 o'clock every Friday but you somehow never manage to let me have it until about lunch-time. This really isn't good enough and I want you to tell me why you can't do what you are supposed to do. What have you got to say for yourself?'

How would you reply to Mrs Thompson? (See the suggested solution.)

Similar care should be taken when speaking to those who consider you to be in authority over them.

TASK 5 (L2)

You are working in a day nursery for pre-school children between the ages of two and five years. The owner tells you to start getting the children ready to go home, so you have to start by getting them to tidy up the nursery, clearing up their toys, putting the rubbish in the bins and arranging all the things that are in the room in an orderly way. How would you go about giving the children that instruction? (See the suggested solution.)

However, things will be a little different when you go to the owner of the day nursery and ask her or him for two days holiday to visit your sick relative in Aberdeen. But, how would you do it? Try and work out a strategy which would be acceptable to the owner (let us call her Mrs Glover), but which would help you to achieve the result you want.

This time do not just think of the words you would use, but also the time and place you would choose to speak.

TASK 6 (L3)

If you adopt the following style, how do you think the owner, Mrs Glover, might react to what you say?

Just as you (Jill/John) and the owner, Mrs Glover, are helping the children put their coats on to go home, and there are mums and dads arriving every few minutes, you casually announce:

> 'By the way, Mrs Glover, I'll be taking two days off next week to go and visit my granny in Aberdeen, because she is very ill.'

You say this without looking at her because you too are busy with the children. (See the suggested solution.)

TASK 7 (L3)

Take a look at the drawing below. Note down as many things as you can about the situation which you think indicate the likelihood of Mrs. Glover refusing the request. Think of how the request should be made to achieve the best result for Jill/John, paying attention to the points which have already been mentioned above. Practise your role play in front of your tutor who will tell you how well or badly you have done. (See the suggested solution.)

Gender differences

This is closely connected to status differences as some women, and a lot of men, think that they are superior to the opposite sex. We should be striving to talk to others according to what we know about their ability, and not to make assumptions about it because of their gender. Bear in mind the points which have been covered up to now and have a look at the next task.

TASK 8 (L2)

Alex, an assistant manager in a busy medium-sized office, wants some work done urgently, so he goes to one of the young female word processor operators and says:

'Hello, Gill, my love, be a good little girl and do this report for me this morning. I need it for an emergency meeting this afternoon.'

Is there anything wrong with the way Alex approached Gill? What do you think Gill's reaction to Alex will be? (See the suggested solution.)

What do you think Gill's reaction to Alex might be?

Directly in the line of fire

This title applies to you if you are one of the people in any organization who give the first impression to any visitors, for example the receptionists in hotels, or at the front desks of buildings, and the people who answer the telephone. Telephone answering techniques will be dealt with a little later, but for the moment, let us look at why it is important that you must choose the right words when you are dealing with visitors.

For a start, you have to put up with anything from pleasant enquiries to abusive demands, not only from the people who come to visit the organization, but from the people who work in it as well.

In order to set the scene, imagine that Mrs Janice Higgins, the Chief Buyer of a large cosmetics distributor, has come to see the Sales Director of a chemical company which supplies the basic products for their cosmetics. Let us call Mrs Higgins' company Arome Products plc, and the Sales Director Mr Wilfred Manning of Anderson-Wells Chemicals Ltd. The receptionist's name is Angela.

TASK 9 (L3)

Read the dialogue below and then answer the questions which follow it, after discussing them with a colleague, or in small groups of two or three:

Angela 'Hello, what can I do for you?'

Mrs Higgins 'My name is Mrs Higgins. I have an appointment with Mr Manning at 10.30.'

Angela 'Mr Merning? I don't think we've got a Mr Merning.'

Mrs Higgins 'Not Merning, Manning. He's your Sales Director.'

Angela 'Oh, right. I know, just a tick. (She telephones an extension.) Cindy, is Wilf around this morning? There's someone here to see him. (pause) I don't know, I'll ask. (turns to Mrs Higgins) Sorry, love, what's your name?'

Mrs Higgins 'Mrs. Higgins. I have an appointment at 10.30.'

Angela (to Cindy) 'It's Mrs Higgins. (pause, turns to Mrs Higgins) She wants to know what company you're from, Mrs Higgins.'

Mrs Higgins 'I'm from Arome Products. I'm the Chief Buyer.'

Angela 'She says she's from At Home Products . . .'

Mrs Higgins (raising her voice) 'Arome, A - R - O - M - E.'

Angela 'She's from Arome Products, silly me. Says she's got an appointment at 10.30. (pause) Do you know where he is then, Cindy? Oh, OK. I'll tell her. (turns to Mrs Higgins) He's in the Lab. Block. It's not far from here. Go out of the main door and turn left. Then turn first left, and go all the way down the passageway. You'll find the Lab. Block on the left at the end. It's got it on the door.'

Mrs Higgins 'Thank you very much for your careful directions. I hope your organization takes better care of the orders that come into this building.'

1 What impression will Mrs Higgins have of Anderson-Wells when she leaves?

2 Has Anderson-Wells' reputation been improved or damaged by the encounter between Angela and Mrs Higgins? State your reasons for your answer.

3 What errors did Angela make in dealing with Mrs Higgins? Make a list of them.

4 What status relationship existed between Angela and Mrs Higgins?

5 What status relationship existed between Anderson-Wells Chemicals and Mrs Higgins, and how should that have affected the way she was treated?

(See the suggested solution.)

There was a marked lack of professionalism about the way Angela dealt with the visitor. The fact that she did not know how important Mrs Higgins was should not have made any difference. If you do not know anything about a visitor, you should treat them as if they are important. Even if they turn out not to be important at all, treat all visitors with courtesy because it is good for the image of the organization.

Never forget, receptionists are the front line image of any organization and should give the best impression possible. The way people are treated by an organization's reception, is the way they are going to remember it in the future.

Now, let us imagine that the meeting between Wilfred Manning and Janice Higgins did not go too well because she was more than a bit put out by the way she had been treated by the receptionist, Angela. There are a number of possible outcomes, such as:

● Mr Manning could have persuaded her to buy his company's products, because he is a good salesman;

● Mrs Higgins could have given him a piece of her mind, and told him she would never consider buying anything from his company, ever again;

● Mr Manning could have been so angry that Angela was given a verbal warning.

All that was required of Angela was a little forethought in how to treat visitors to the company and any bad feeling could have been avoided. After all, it is difficult enough to find and keep customers in a competitive market, without it being made worse through thoughtless behaviour by employees towards customers.

To emphasize what is good conduct, work in small groups in class, and rewrite the dialogue between the receptionist, Angela, and Mrs Higgins so that, at the end of it you can honestly give positive responses to questions 1 and 2 in Task 9. The final result should be checked with your tutor.

Now we move on to discuss choosing the right words and tone. You cannot proceed to this until you are clear of your situation and your relationship with the person to whom you are speaking.

If you know the person already, then problems will be few, although it is worth remembering that if you know the person only in a particular situation, e.g. at work, he or she may behave differently towards you under different circumstances, e.g. on holiday, at a party, etc. However, in the work situation the element of surprise at someone's change in behaviour arises very rarely. It is usually as a result of people being given new responsibilities, or even promotion.

 TASK 10 (L3)

Why do people change their otherwise familiar behaviour pattern in such circumstances? List as many reasons as you can think of which would explain such behaviour. (See the suggested solution.)

If you don't know the people with whom you are speaking, you must pay close attention to their way of behaving, that is,

- the way they speak;
- the way they dress;
- the way they act.

A stranger's way of behaving is totally unfamiliar to us and we have to make a meaningful assessment of it. We have no background information on which to draw. Our experience and impressions begin from the first meeting.

Choosing the right words

Here is another situation for you to think about. Mr Tony Bold is a first - class industrial chemist who has been running his own business for five years. His business provides a highly specialised analytical service to chemical manufacturers. The manufacturers would need the service only on an occasional basis, and so it is cheaper for them to employ the services of Tony's company as and when they need the service, rather than to employ someone full-time with the skill to carry out the tests. As with many companies, however, business has become more competitive, and so Tony thinks it's time to clarify a few points before things go too far by talking to his small work-force, most of whom are laboratory trained. This is what he says to them:

> *'It has come to my notice that our ROC ratios have dropped to levels which are no longer acceptable to the directors of the firm and it has therefore become necessary to re-appraise productivity in every area of the firm. In addition to that, budget allocations will have to be reviewed to offset imbalances which, up to now, we have been able to absorb, but which in fact lead to some overspending in areas where reductions could easily be attained without adversely affecting productivity in other areas where the improvement in profits would enhance the ROC. In order to achieve that objective I have set up the necessary machinery and hope to receive your full co-operation.'*

TASK 11 (L3)

All that you have to do now is to try and work out what Tony Bold was talking about! This will not be an easy task because he is using language which is more in keeping with the style he might use when talking to his accountant. So, by way of giving you some help, it will be useful to tell you that ROC means a return on the capital employed in an organization. Put in more simple terms, if you put £100 into your Post Office Savings Account and left it there for a year, you would receive, say £5 from the Post Office at the end of that time. This is called 'interest' but in business the capital is not cash, but the investment in buildings, equipment, raw materials and everything else used to produce the products or services of the enterprise, and represented in the company accounts in money values.

Another point that should be made, is that Tony Bold's purpose in speaking to his work-force is to tell them that some changes will have to be made, and what these changes will mean to them. Obviously he has not done this. What you should be trying to do, is to unravel his talk and put it into the kind of language that will mean something to his employees. This is a difficult task, especially if you have little or no experience of the business world, but try your best. (See the suggested solution.)

The spoken word is probably the most important means of communication in the work place, and it is equally important when people in different organizations want to communicate by telephone. The example of Mr Bold highlights the importance of choosing the right language for your audience. It is irrelevant how important the message is. If the language is not appropriate, the message will not be heard.

People use 'technical' words, jargon, dialect, idiomatic phrases and situational words and phrases which are used in some circumstances, but are inappropriate in others. Then there is 'swearing', or 'bad language', as it is sometimes called. No dictionary can tell you how and when it should be used, because it is often anti-social, while in some situations it is expected.

Accents

Hardly any other topic relating to language arouses as much passion as accents. While they are often the focus of amusement in other countries, just as they are in the United Kingdom, accents are seldom used as weapons of inferiority to the extent that they are in this country. For example, in Germany, people speak two kinds of German: low German, which is a regional accent or dialect, and high German, which is a kind of standard German, universally accepted and understood by all German speakers. People quite happily speak both kinds of German, depending on the situation they are in.

However, in the United Kingdom, accents are often used to place people in their proper social class, most accents being seen as inferior to what people call 'received pronunciation', or RP. This is the kind of upper class accent associated with the southern part of the country and spoken by the Queen and most people who have been educated at public school.

This begs the question, 'Do we have to get rid of our accents if we are to be successful in our careers?' The answer is clearly 'No', otherwise people like Cilla Black, Terry Wogan and Derek Jameson would never have made it anywhere. However, accents *can* be a burden to some of us.

The question is, 'If we have an accent, what do we do about it?' Before trying to answer this troubled question, it should be made clear that nowadays many linguistic experts consider RP to be just as much of an accent as Scouse (Liverpool, for those who do not know). For those of us who have regional accents, there is the complication that some of them are more acceptable than others. Then there is the problem of the accent which is almost beyond comprehension to those who are not familiar with it. The tactic which anyone who has any accent at all should adopt, is to try to abandon its worst extremes. This means that strong, local pronunciations of words should be honed into more easily understood ones.

It is very difficult to print examples, as there are only twenty-six letters in the alphabet, but there are nearly fifty spoken sounds in English. As well as the numerous British accents there are a great many more in the rest of the world.

The clear message to all of us with accents is: do not try to lose your accent; simply try to make sure that your accent is not a barrier to communication for those who do not share it.

TASK 12 (L3)

The class, or group, with whom you are studying should take a cassette recorder with them and go into the street, or make appointments to visit people from different social classes, and interview them about their accents. Draw up a short questionnaire which will highlight the difficulties and advantages of speaking with a regional accent which is not from the area in which the interviewee is now living.

Give details of the accent of each interviewee and whether he or she has tempered it together with their reasons for doing so. There is no suggested solution to this task, but it can be assessed by asking your tutor to look at your questionnaire and analysis of the answers you obtained from it.

Slovenly speech

Slovenly speech is something which is found no matter what accent a person has, and should be avoided at all costs. Speaking in a slovenly way involves three main areas of speech:

- incorrect grammar and syntax;
- bad pronunciation;
- improper use of words.

TASK 13 (L2)

Here is an example of someone who clearly does not care about making all three mistakes in the one sentence:

> *'I told him, see, we wasn't going to except anythink less nor the pay raise we ast for in the first place.'*

Test your knowledge of good English by finding an example of each one of the faults mentioned above. When you think you have done that, write them down and then make an evaluation of the kind of impression you think the sentence would have on:

a a peer group;

b a member of the senior management team.

(See the suggested solution.)

The lessons to be drawn from the above example are:

- that slovenly speech should not be confused with accent;
- that most of us make some grammatical errors in spoken language, but not enough to be called slovenly;
- that the way we speak, i.e., accent or slovenliness, can result in our exclusion from some social, work or professional groups.

It should also be pointed out that very correct, grammatical speech could be a barrier to any progress in some work situations, whereas in others it is a positive advantage.

Using the right tone of voice

Tone of voice, or *intonation*, as it is sometimes called, is very important in English, because it can give a meaning to a sentence which is sometimes impossible to achieve with words alone. In written English, the intonation often has to be explained, but when it involves no more than emphasis, the stressed words are usually written in italics.

TASK 14 (L2)

Below is a short sentence which is written the same way four times, but with different words stressed each time. You have to rewrite the sentences in such a way as to show what the difference in meaning is between them.

1 **You're** not going to wear that hat.

2 You're **not** going to wear that hat.

3 You're not going to **wear** that hat.

4 You're not going to wear **that** hat.

(See the suggested solution.)

Now that stress has been highlighted you will no doubt be able to recognize it in much of what both yourself, and other people, say. Of course, it is not only the stress on words which gives deeper meaning to what we say.

Intonation is used extensively in television advertising 'voice-overs' in order to associate the product being advertised with a particular quality. This is expressed through the speaker's voice. For example, where the advertiser wants to suggest the softness, or gentleness, of a product, the voice-over will adopt a soothing tone, and, at the same time, use persuasive language to give you information about the product. This device has been used so often that people are quite used to it, and quite aware of what the advertisers are doing, but the fact that they keep doing it suggests that it still works.

Another device which advertisers use, is to adopt two contrasting styles of intonation in the same advertisement. This has the effect of making us sit up and take notice, but it only works when there is an element of surprise. Once people become familiar with the particular advert, the device loses its impact.

The point of the next exercise is to make you aware of how the differences in your voice can help you to express different attitudes and meanings to suit the occasion. You may also notice that with each intonation there is also a change in sentence construction, as well as the words used.

To illustrate this point, consider the following example.

Harry Dean is the sales manager of Highfield Leisure Ltd, a company which markets several brands of leisure and fitness equipment. Although the company sells to customers all over the UK, Harry has always wanted to have greater penetration of the Scottish market. As the result of a new sales initiative, he has at last made three useful contacts in the Glasgow area. To maintain the momentum, he agrees to go up to Glasgow at the earliest opportunity, which is the following day and the day after. Everything else can be put off until he gets back. He has to take his demonstration kit with him in a suitable vehicle, and have accommodation in a hotel with lock-up facilities, as well as a room which can be used for the demonstrations. The demonstrations are scheduled for Wednesday and Thursday, so, on Tuesday morning, Harry says to his Personal Assistant, Maisie Andrews:

> *'Maisie, I'm going to Glasgow tonight. I've managed to arrange three demonstrations there on Wednesday and Thursday. Book me a hotel room in a place with the usual facilities for tonight and tomorrow. Make sure the kit is in the company van and that it's ready to go about four. If there are any problems let me know on the mobile phone. See you later this afternoon.'*

Intonation. Harry shot the words out like bullets, each sentence being like a command. The shortness of the sentences adds to the urgency which Harry wishes to convey, and they are unencumbered by politeness.

Situation. The relationship between Harry and Maisie is a close working one, and each knows the other so well that Harry's style does not offend her.

TASK 15 (L3)

Look at five television adverts of your own choice, and try to choose some which are very different from each other. To prepare for the task ahead it might be advisable to familiarize yourself with a range of attitudes and feelings which can be expressed through the intonation of the voices used in the advertisements. Here are some ideas:

enthusiasm	persuasion	urgency
concern	friendliness	anger
happiness	dominance	compliance

To the above examples, add your own ideas, and then try to think of a recent occasion when you expressed them. If you have any difficulty in linking an attitude to an occasion, then talk it over with a friend or colleague. Resort to an imaginary situation, if necessary. For each advertisement:

- What message is the advertisement trying to get across to viewers?
- What intonation of voice is being used and how does it help to strengthen the message of the advertisement?
- Are there any other features of the voice used in the voice-over which play a significant part in getting the message across?

It would help the rest of your group if you could put the advertisements onto video and play them back in class. Ask the group for their opinions on the intonation used in the advertisements. To help them, let them have the checklist you used when you watched. Compare your findings by putting them on to a flip chart or large white board so that the whole spectrum of opinion can be seen at a glance.

There is no suggested solution to this exercise as the choice of advertisements that people make is bound to be very varied.

TASK 16 (L2/3)

Look at the photographs on page 21 and then write down what you think the people are like (e.g. their accent, occupation, hobbies, whether or not they are married, and even what newspaper they read). Obviously much of what you write will be pure speculation, but that does not mean that it will be wrong. Of course, it may not always be right either! (See the suggested solution.)

(a)   (b)   (c)   (d)

Fig. 1 First impressions

Listening with understanding

Listening with understanding is not always as obvious as it seems. Just because someone says something to us does not necessarily mean we are bound to understand them, even though we can hear what they have said quite clearly. Most of us know how true this can be. How often have you been in the position where you have not understood a thing that has been said? Let's just check up on a few details first, you might say to yourself. The other person is speaking English, I can hear what they are saying quite clearly, but I do not understand their meaning.

There is a saying which describes that state of affairs: It's Greek to me. This simply means that we cannot understand what the other person has said.

TASK 17 (L2/3)

Note down as many reasons as you can think of why it should be difficult for someone to understand what you have just said to them.(See the suggested solution.)

The reasons given in the solution to the last task referred to the way you, *the speaker*, went about constructing what you wanted to say. There may be other reasons for a lack of understanding, however, which refer to how you, *the listener*, go about the task of listening.

When you listen to someone speak, there are, very basically, three processes which your brain has to go through.

1   It recognizes the meanings of the words being spoken;

2   It recognizes patterns of language such as tenses and questions;

3   It takes account of stress, intonation and the body language of the speaker.

The actual process is much more complicated than that, but it would not add anything significant to the purpose of this book to include further details here.

Let us assume that the reasons mentioned above were not the ones which prevented understanding, but that the reason was something which the listener did or did not do? The simplest way of explaining the lack of understanding is to say that the listener did not concentrate, but such an explanation is not specific enough if we are to use it as a means of improving our ability to understand what others say.

TASK 18 (L2)

Working in small groups of two or three, make a list of as many reasons as you can think of why you might not be able to understand what someone else says to you, even when they are speaking your language! (See the suggested solution.)

You will probably find that your answers for tasks 17 and 18 overlap.

If things are as serious as this, then there must be something we can do to make sure that any failure to understand what someone is saying to us is not our fault. Understanding can be helped by employing a number of techniques:

1   Listen for the key words of the conversation.

2   Listen for the common thread, if there are a number of pieces of information included in the same conversation.

3   Do not think of anything else of importance at the same time, which might affect your ability to concentrate.

4   Do not make assumptions when you are unsure about the meaning of some word, phrase, or idea.

5   Do not be afraid to ask for clarification of meaning at any time.

6   If the person who has been talking to you does not do it, make sure you summarize what you think has been said to you, and obtain agreement from that person.

Effective listening and understanding what has been said are nothing more than an exercise in comprehension or summarizing, except that it is done with the spoken word.

Before you attempt the next task, look at the section on summarizing in Chapter 2. This might help you to make meaningful notes as you listen to the piece being read, or even if you are watching a television or radio broadcast.

TASK 19 (L2)

The following exercise, highlights what it means to understand what other people have said to you.

A manager came into the office one day, and said to his secretary, who was fairly new to the job:

> *'Jennifer, would you make sure that the minutes of the last meeting of the Board of Directors are done within the next two days, that's Wednesday. Send a copy to all the directors, there are six of them, don't forget, including the new one who lives in Carlisle. While you're at it, enclose a blank expenses form with each one, as there is always somebody who forgets to do it at the meeting. The minutes have to be printed on the good quality paper, and sent out in the good-looking envelopes, not the brown ones. And don't forget the compliments slips with each one either.'*

Try giving these instructions to another group member and see how much they are able to remember. Then ask him or her if there are any questions a relatively new secretary might like to ask after receiving a list of instructions like the one above. Make sure that you have thought out the kinds of information a new secretary might like to have, before you attempt the exercise. (See the suggested solution.)

TASK 20 (L2/3)

You may have thought of a few more points than those suggested; if so, well done. What then, should Jennifer do about those things which she knows very little about? Obviously, she should ask the appropriate questions, which will produce the answers she needs to do the job correctly. Use the list of queries from Task 19 to construct the appropriate questions. Remember that the questions must be framed in such a way as to produce an informative answer. In such a situation, it is often useful to say that you are not sure of something, or that there is something your superior evidently thinks needs no explanation. (See the suggested solution.)

TASK 21 (L2)

Although the points of information and the questions to be asked seem to be fairly simple, can you make a list of the things that might have gone wrong if Jennifer had not asked them? (See the suggested solution.)

Sometimes speed is very important because of the urgency of the task which has to be tackled. This puts an additional strain on the need to concentrate on getting the correct meaning from messages.

TASK 22 (L3)

Imagine you are a trainee accountant and that the major part of your work consists of auditing clients' accounts at their premises. One morning the principle partner in the firm, Mr Jones, gives you some verbal instructions as he is rushing out of the office. He speaks quickly while he is walking to the door, and part of what he says is drowned by a noise from the street.

> 'George, I'm off to Pickering's, but you'll have to go to Robinson's of Chester for me, to do an emergency audit. Someone is supposed to be there now, so I want you to drop what you're doing, pass it on to Wendy to finish, and go to Robinson's today. Don't go the Church Street way, there's been an accident and it's jammed solid. When you get there, start with their purchase ledger, and pay particular attention to all of the capital items purchased because so . . . (loud noise) . . . flated figure. I don't think some of the directors expenses are entirely correct either, so check them carefully.'

Obviously there are two possibilities open to you which will make the exercise more like the real situation described above.

1 The first option is to get someone to act the part of Mr Jones. The person should read the passage once, very quickly, without going back on even one word.

2 You can read the passage carefully and go back over any points you missed.

Make up your mind which option you are going to choose before reading the passage, and then answer the following questions.

a What are the key words in Mr Jones' spoken instructions?

b Can you guess what was said by him when he was drowned out by the noise?

c What, if any, is the common theme running through what he said?

(See the suggested solution.)

Apart from the solution to the above task, it is important to remember some of the points which were made earlier, about how to behave in certain situations.

It is important not to be afraid to ask for explanations, or to ask questions that might clear up any misunderstandings. The fact that Mr Jones says his piece as he is heading for the door, and in a great hurry, should not deter you from your purpose. That purpose is that you should know exactly what he means. It is also necessary to clear up the problem of the external noise which seems to have obliterated part of what Mr Jones had to say. Bearing those two points in mind, it is essential that you stop him from leaving before he explains the points you are not clear about.

Even if you think you know exactly what he means, and that you think you know what he said when a noise prevented you from hearing it, you must make the effort to summarize your understanding of what you think he means. That way there can be no possibility of you acting on an assumption.

Try out how effective your powers of listening are by attempting the following task. Before you attempt it, you must make up your mind to be absolutely honest. No sneaking a look at the written word beforehand!

TASK 23 (L3)

The exercise should be carried out in five stages.

Stage 1

Each member of the group, or class, has to find an article of considerable complexity in a magazine such as *The Economist*, *Time*, *Newsweek*, *The Spectator*, *Management Today* or any other which carries articles of some depth and difficulty.

Stage 2

When you have found one, go through it carefully several times to make sure that you have understood it thoroughly, and make a list of all the main points in it. If you are not sure whether it is suitable or not, check with your tutor, but do not ask him/her to tell you if you have got all the main points down yet.

Stage 3

Practise reading the article making sure that you use the correct tone of voice for its content.

Stage 4

Choose a partner from the group or class and read the article to him/her once or twice only, asking him/her to summarize the main points of the piece.

Stage 5

Compare the list of main points made by your partner with those which you made and discuss any omissions or other differences.

A variation on this theme would be to choose a television programme, or radio broadcast, of a debate of some depth on a topic which has not been openly discussed in other areas of the media. Such programmes are usually found on Channel 4, BBC2, Radio 3 or Radio 4.

There is no suggested solution to Task 23 as there can be no way of knowing what magazine article, television or radio programme you might choose. Provided your tutor agrees to do it, ask him/her to go over the article or broadcast to make sure that you have identified the correct points as being the main ones.

Talking on the telephone

When we talk to others, we find it useful to be aware of their facial and other body movements in order to have a complete picture of what people really mean and feel when they are talking to us. In short, what people do with their eyes, face and general body posture gives the recipient of someone else's communication additional information which is not otherwise available. In some cases the message which comes from what people say does not match up with the message which comes from their body language.

That extra information is not available when we talk on the telephone; we have only the spoken words and the intonation of the speaker's voice to guide us. This means that both the caller and the person receiving the call have to be extra vigilant to be sure that the information itself, and the level of understanding between the two people, are neither misunderstood nor misinterpreted. This seems like a pretty tall order, especially as the chances of not getting the message right are fairly high, even when two people are talking to each other face-to-face.

Telephone calls take two forms:

- the ones you make yourself, and
- the ones you receive.

Let's start by looking at the telephone calls you initiate: that means, the ones you make yourself.

Making telephone calls

Before making a telephone call, there are three things you should be sure of, unless, of course, it is an emergency:

1   Who do you want to speak to?
2   What are you going to say to that person?
3   When are you going to make the call, i.e. the time of day?

Who do you want to speak to?
All too often we make calls to other organizations, for private or for business purposes, without even asking the name of the person we have been

speaking to. Even when we ask who it is, we often forget the name, or we forget to write it down, then and there. Quite a lot of the time this is not a problem, because the person concerned does what you have asked them to do, and knowing their name would not have made it happen any faster. However, there are occasions when we expect the organization concerned to have provided us with some service or other, or to have sent us goods or equipment, and nothing happens, or a mistake is made. Without contact names or reference numbers, we cannot get satisfaction quickly. There is no faceless person, called Arthur, or Agnes, at the other end of the telephone to whom we can complain.

Getting hold of the right person on the telephone is not always straight-forward. It is all too easy for someone who answers the telephone to think:

> *'Oh, no! I don't want to spend time dealing with this problem, I've got enough to do.'*

He or she will then make every attempt to pass you on to another person, preferably on another extension number. For the caller there is nothing worse than being transferred to numerous different extensions and hav-ing to repeat the enquiry details, in full, each time another person cheerily asks, 'Hello, my name's Cyril. How can I help you?' and then promptly proceeds not to!

The secret is to have the name of the right person before you make the call in the first place. Even then, your call will more than likely not go as well as it does in almost every film and TV programme, where the caller calls someone, that person answers the call immediately, and the problem is resolved, or arrangements are made. In reality, most calls result in:

- an engaged tone,
- no reply, or
- 'I'm sorry, he/she isn't here at the moment.'

TASK 24 (L2)

In the first two cases the solution is simply to try again. But the solution to the third is not so easy. What would you do? Think about this for a few minutes, and then make a decision, because there is more than one possibility. If you are working with a class or some other group, put everyone's ideas on to a flip chart or white board, and discuss them openly. (See the suggested solution.)

Knowing the name of the person we want to speak to is a great help, but it is not an 'open sesame' to the information you are trying to find out. With perseverance, you should be able to contact them in the end.

Your troubles are doubled, however, when you do not have the name of the person you want to speak to, because finding that information out can be very tricky, especially in a large organization. In fact, some large organizations seem to discourage callers from finding out the name of one person who can be contacted.

What are you going to say?

The most important aspect of making a telephone call is knowing what you are going to say once you have made contact with the right person, or at least with the right department. Time is money, especially when your call is twice as long as it needs to be as a result of bad planning. There is also the possibility that you are going to be unsuccessful in getting someone to agree to what you are going to ask them to do, so have an alternative strategy you can switch to if you have to. If a certain outcome is essential, make sure you achieve it and if you cannot, make sure that you know why not.

Another source of time wasting on the telephone is idle chit-chat, sometimes mistakenly called 'small talk'. It certainly will not look small when the telephone bill comes in! Your employer, or yourself if you are self-employed, pays for that time twice. Once, because your time is expensive, and a second time because telephone calls are expensive.

Some incidental chatting is to be expected as it is part of normal human behaviour. It also helps us to establish a rapport with our contact in the organization we are calling. Such a relationship can be advantageous when we want someone to do us a special favour. It can also be useful for smoothing the way if things go wrong.

However, a good reason for not indulging in small talk is that the person you are calling might be busy and want to get on with his or her work. The recipient will not mind dealing with your call so much if it gets to the point quickly, but if too much of his or her time is being spent on non-work, this can be quite irritating.

Bad planning and mere 'chat' may also have the effect of confusing the person you have called, so that it takes even longer to get the information or action you wanted from the call in the first place.

When are you going to call?

The time of day when you make the call might also be of some importance. Calls made during business hours are more expensive, so avoid making inessential calls then. Good times to phone to make sure that people do not want to chat are:

- just before lunch when people are hungry, and
- just before the end of the working day, when people want to finish up before going home.

A guide to making effective calls

Bear in mind the points which were made earlier in this chapter about status and gender differences, and the need to present the right image of the organization you are working for, to others.

The following checklist will help you to make more effective calls.

1   First of all, listen to what is said when your call is answered. You may have got through to the wrong place.

2   Then say, 'Good morning/afternoon, may I speak to . . . please, on extension . . .'

3   When you get through to the extension, ask, 'Is that . . . ? Good morning/afternoon. My name is . . . of . . . I'd like to ask/tell you/ speak to you about . . .'

4   If the person you wanted to speak to is not there, someone may offer to take a message. You may leave the message, or, if that is not suitable, ask him/her to call you back. But remember to leave your number, name, and firm.

5   If you would rather telephone the person you have called, ask, 'Could you tell me the best time to reach . . . ?'

Remember, at all times, when you are on the telephone, be sure to have a pad and pen by the telephone to take down any details which you want to know. They soon slip from your memory as you continue with your call.

How well do you plan your telephone calls? If you are not very sure, try out the following task.

TASK 25 (L2/3)

Draw up a Telephone Call Record Sheet and keep it by your phone. Every time you make a call, fill in the details and, at the end of the day, add up the totals. To help you out, a suggested plan appears below.

TELEPHONE CALL RECORD SHEET

Number called	Charge band	Start time	Finish time	Chatting time	Business time	Total

There is no suggested solution to this exercise. It is left to your own common sense to judge whether you are spending too much time chatting and not enough on business.

A simple analysis of the time you spend on non-work conversation in the course of a day's telephone calls can then be converted into money value, and you will then be able to see how expensive such conversation really is. The results of this exercise may come as a surprise.

When you have carried out the above task, the next stage is to set about reorganizing the way you prepare your telephone calls.

- Make sure you know who you are going to speak to.
- Write down exactly what you want to say/ask.
- Write down what outcome you want from the call.
- Prioritize your calls in terms of urgency and expense.

- Decide on the time of day when you will make the call, and if you have a lot of calls to make in a day, set aside a certain time of day when they can all be made at once.

- When you have completed the business of the call, finish the conversation as quickly as it is polite to do so.

TASK 26 (L2)

Go through the above checklist for every call you make, using the telephone call record sheet, or whatever system you have devised for yourself. Cover the same period of time as you did the first time you used the sheet and make a note to see if the time you spend on the telephone has been more productive. Note any differences and explain them.

You will have noticed that you have to spend some time going through your checklist before each call, but this should speed up the more you become used to the routine, and will not add much time to your telephone time.

There is no model answer to this task, but it will be useful to compare your results with others in your group. Those of you who have not yet joined the ranks of the employed could try it out at home with only slight adaptation. You will then be able to show whoever pays the bills how much money you have saved them by limiting your calls!

Receiving telephone calls

Receiving telephone calls involves an entirely different set of problems because you have no idea who is going to call you, or at what time of day they will do so. Luckily, when you first start work you will probably be in a fairly junior position, and any calls you receive will be routine in nature. However, this does not mean that you should treat them lightly. Every call that comes into an organization has certain implications:

- The caller has expectations about its outcome; and
- the treatment the caller receives on the telephone leaves him/her with an impression of the organization.

Go back to Task 9 and see what was said about someone speaking to a visitor to the firm. All you have to do is to put yourself in a similar position and imagine that you are the person on the other end of the line by responding to others.

How to handle incoming calls

If you are on reception and you answer an incoming call, you must do your best to sound cheerful, positive, polite, and ready to deal with any enquiry that is likely to be put to you, so start with a salutation and an offer to help, such as this:

'Good morning, Super Enterprises. Kevin Dowell speaking. May I help you?'

If you are answering a telephone extension in a department, the only change should be that the name of the organization is substituted for the name of your department or section.

The following checklist might be of use:

1   If the caller asks to be put through to an extension, simply do so.
2   If the caller asks to be put through to a particular person, make sure that you have understood the name correctly. After all, there could be more than one person with the same (or similar) name.
3   If there is no reply to the extension, go back and tell the caller. The caller then has the opportunity to ask for someone else, or for another extension number.
4   Never leave the caller hanging on, listening to an extension ringing out in vain. There is nothing more annoying.
5   If you are trying to find the information the caller has asked for but are finding it difficult, keep going back to the telephone to let him or her know that you have not forgotten about the call. It is also a good idea to say that you will call him or her back when you have found the information, if it is taking a long time to find. This shows consideration for the other person's time and telephone bill!
6   When a customer is angry about something, the first thing you should do is to make a simple apology, and try to find the person who can best deal with his or her complaint.
7   No matter how personal the attack on you is, do not be tempted to fight back. Keep calm and stay polite. Reassure the caller that you are doing all you can to help him or her.

TASK 27 (L2/3)

Look at the following situations which involve answering the telephone, and decide what you would say in each case. When you have done so, act out the situations in front of the group. When everyone has done this, discuss them as a group and see what you can learn from each other's mistakes.

Situation 1

You have worked for your company for six years and you are on the switchboard when a call comes in for the Managing Director, Mr Grossman. Mr Grossman's calls are being redirected to his secretary's extension, which usually means that he is in a meeting. As his secretary's extension is engaged at the moment, you tell the caller that Mr Grossman is busy, but the caller says that it is a matter of great urgency. What would you do?

Situation 2

You are on the switchboard when someone who is coming for an interview phones up to say that he is lost. Using the location of your place of work, school or college, how would you help the caller to find the place, allowing only fifteen minutes for the journey?

Situation 3

An important customer has an appointment with your boss at 10 am but he phones up at 9.30 am to say his car has broken down about two miles away. Again, use the location of your place of work, school or college, and say how you would help the customer to get to his appointment as quickly as possible. Think of as many alternatives as possible.

Situation 4

It is 9.45 am and you are working in your department, alone, when a colleague rings up to say that he is sick and will not be at work that day. You are certain that this is not true, because you saw him that morning on the train on the way to work. Do you relay his message without comment, or do you tell your boss what you saw. Give your reasons.

Situation 5

You are working in the export department of your company which makes electronic components for a wide range of products. A customer in Kenya phones and is very angry that some urgently required components have not been delivered by air freight as promised. He wants you to make sure that they will be delivered no later than the following day. What do you say to the customer, and how do you handle his angrily delivered demand? You have to telephone him back in an hour at Nairobi 61245. Who would you have to contact to find out if you could meet his demands? What details would you need to pass on to the customer? Assume that you are able to get his order to him the next day, what is the full number you would dial, and what would you say to the customer?

Situation 6

You and your manager are going to Norwich for two days and she asks you to get two train tickets for the day after tomorrow, and also to arrange hotel accommodation for two nights for the two of you. Your firm has an account with a local travel agent, and you normally stay at the Royal Norfolk Hotel in Norwich. What questions would you ask your manager before booking anything, and what would you say to:

a the travel agent, and

b the hotel?

(See the suggested solutions.)

A summary of the main points

- Telephone calls rely on words, stress and intonation, only.
- Know who you are going to speak to.
- Plan what you are going to say and how you are going to say it.
- Leave messages only if you think the person will call you back.
- When someone is not there, find out a time when they are most likely to be there, and call them at that time.
- Talk to other people only when you think they will be able to help.
- Whether making a call, or receiving one, always be polite.
- Any information you are given on the telephone should be written down immediately.
- Always check that you have got the right information by repeating it to the person on the other end of the line. The same goes for any agreement that has been made.
- Telephone calls are expensive. Keep them brief by planning them.
- If you cannot answer a telephone enquiry, refer it to someone who can, or offer to call back.
- If callers are angry, do not argue with them, try to calm them down and reassure them that you will help them.

Telephone messages

The standard of telephone message taking in most organizations is very poor. Somehow or other, messages do not get through, or they are misunderstood or otherwise mishandled.

There are a few simple rules which everyone should note, no matter where they are employed, and which will help to keep potential customers, or any other callers, much happier.

1 Every telephone should have a standard message pad and a pencil beside it.
2 Everyone should have a place where telephone messages are left. It should be clearly identified as such.
3 Everyone in the organization should be trained in how to take a telephone message.

TASK 28 (L2)

Bearing in mind what has been said above about telephone messages, design what you think would be an ideal message pad. (See the suggested solution.)

If your organization has staff training sessions on a regular basis, one of the items which should appear on the agenda from time to time is, how to take down telephone messages. They should always be short, even when the caller has gone into a long and detailed account of why he/she is phoning in the first place. When you have taken the message down, always check with the caller that your summary is what he/she has said. The message should be written down as soon as it has been given to you to ensure that it is correct. The longer you wait before writing the message down, the less likely it is that you will do so accurately.

TASK 29 (L2)

You are a junior manager in the administration section of a large general hospital and on returning to your office from a meeting one afternoon, you find the following message on your desk:

Telephone Message

TIME RECEIVED_____   DATE_____

FROM_____

Mr Andrews phoned from Reading to
make enquiries about visiting you on
Friday. Could you phone back to
Confirm details. He says you know
his number.

RECEIVED BY_Angela_____

Angela was a temp who has since left the hospital. Her agency was Open Book Temps and your contact there is Sylvia Conway. Write a short report on how you would deal with the badly recorded telephone message. Your report should start with a statement about what was wrong with the original message. (See the suggested solution.)

2
Writing it down

This chapter covers Elements 2.2 and 3.2

The overall aim of Elements 2.2 and 3.2 is to ensure that students will be able to prepare written material on a range of routine and other matters.

OBJECTIVES

At the end of the elements, students will be able to provide written material on a range of routine and other matters, and the information included:

1 is necessary, accurate and appropriate to the purpose and needs of the audience;

2 is presented in documents which are legible;

3 uses grammar and punctuation which follow standard conventions, and words which are spelled correctly;

4 is in a format which is appropriate to the nature of the material and is ordered appropriately to maximize audience understanding.

The rules of writing

The problem with English grammar is that few people know anything about it, at least, that is what people say. It is not true, of course, and we know that because almost everyone whose native language is English speaks it using the rules of grammar, even though they could not write many of them down. They have internalized them, and use them without having to think what they are.

The rules of grammar, after all, were written down after the language was developed, and they change from time to time, as the language continues to develop.

In trying to put things into some kind of order, a set of 'names', or 'vocabulary', had to be developed in order to describe the various functions which words had. Let us look at some of them now.

Nouns

Nouns are the names we give to things. This is not always as simple as it looks, because nouns in turn fall into the following categories:

Common nouns

Examples of these would include hill, street, tree, dog, car and television. These are the names of things which we recognize, and we can even draw them, if we wanted to.

Abstract nouns

These give names to ideas and concepts such as love, beauty, poverty, honesty, ability and laziness.

Proper nouns

These put a name to unique individual people or things like Birmingham, China, William or the Mersey. They are distinguished from other nouns by the fact that they always begin with a capital letter no matter where they are in the sentence.

Collective nouns

As if three categories of nouns were not enough, there are groups of words called collective nouns, such as a *pack* of wolves, a *bevy* of beauties, a *flock* of sheep or a *team* of horses. However, although we use them to describe groups of people, animals or things, these nouns are usually treated as singular when they are put together with a verb. For example:

There is a pack of wolves over there.

However, if we wanted to talk about wolves in general, we would say:

There are wolves in the forest.

 TASK 30 (L2)

Read the following passage and pick out all the nouns which appear in it. List them under the headings: nouns, proper nouns and collective nouns.

When Janice entered her office on Monday morning, she was surprised to see a brand new desk with a bunch of flowers in a vase on it.

(See the suggested solution.)

Pronouns

Pronouns are words which replace nouns in a way which helps to shorten our sentences and make them less clumsy.

Example 1

Mr Andrews, the sales representative, came in the door. Mr Andrews spoke to the receptionist.

can be reduced to:

He spoke to the receptionist.

Example 2

The receptionist asked Mr Andrews for his name.

can be reduced to:

She asked him for his name.

In Example 1 'Mr Andrews, the sales representative' has been replaced by 'he', and in Example 2 'The receptionist' has been replaced by 'She', and 'Mr Andrews' by 'him'. The two sentences could be linked together by the conjunction 'and', in this way:

Mr Andrews, the sales representative, spoke to the receptionist and she asked him for his name.

Personal pronouns

These perform particular functions in representing people, animals and things in sentences, so that they do not have to be named over and over again. (See Examples 1 and 2 above.) But they also change their form according to the function they are performing in a sentence. A simple sentence would be:

William swims.

It can be reduced to:

He swims.

Where the *subject* of the sentence is replaced by a personal pronoun, the following are used:

I, you, he, she, it, we, you, they

Where the personal pronoun is used to replace the *object* of the sentence, the following are used:

me, you, him, her, it, us, you, them

Where the personal pronoun is used to indicate absolute possession, the following are used:

mine, yours, his, hers, its, ours, yours, theirs

Where the personal pronoun is used to indicate the indirect object, the following are used:

(to) me, (to) you, (to) him, her, it, (to) us, (to) you, (to) them

There are other words which look like personal pronouns, but these are really adjectives representing the possessive case:

my, your, his, her, its, our, your, their

Demonstrative pronouns

There is also the demonstrative pronoun, which is used to point out people or objects. These are:

this, that, these, those

Reflexive pronouns

Reflexive pronouns show that the action carried out by the subject, or the 'doer' in the sentence, comes back on him or her. For example:

I'll do it myself.

These are simply object pronouns with the addition of the suffix '-self':

myself, yourself, himself, herself, itself, ourselves, yourselves, themselves

Reflexive pronouns are not always used in the same way as they are in the last example, however. They are sometimes used as *emphatic* pronouns to stress the person doing or receiving an action:

I'll see to it myself.
Make sure you do it yourself.

Interrogative pronouns

In sentences which are questions, we can avoid the use of cumbersome nouns by replacing them with interrogative pronouns:

Which city is it?   *Where is it?*

Which person in this room did it?   *Who did it?*

Which of the things in the shop do you want?   *What do you want?*

The interrogative pronouns are:

who, whom, what, where, when, which, whose

Relative pronouns

Another form of pronoun is the relative pronoun, which makes the link between a noun which has already been mentioned in a sentence, and some additional information about that noun. The main relative pronouns are:

who, whom, which, that

These are used in the following way:

The people who came for lunch yesterday enjoyed their meal.

The star whom we all love to hate is on television again.

The plane which has just landed has flown non-stop from Hong Kong.

The car that you wanted to see has just been sold.

In many cases the relative pronoun is left out of the sentence, especially when the information referring to the noun comes immediately after it:

The flat (that) you wanted to rent is no longer to let.

TASK 31 (L2)

Read the passage which appears below and pick out all the pronouns grouping them into the following categories: pronouns; personal pronouns; interrogative pronouns; demonstrative pronouns; reflexive pronouns and relative pronouns.

Alex looked enviously at Clive's new mountain bike. He would give anything to own one just like it and be able to go off cycling, who knows where? If only he didn't have to study, he could get a part-time job and save up for his own bike. Anyway, it was nobody's fault but his own. If only he had studied a bit harder last year he would have been able to work and save for one, and he would be able to please himself what he did in his spare time. That was the problem, his own laziness. It was his lack of ability to knuckle down which was to blame for his misery.

(See the suggested solution.)

Adjectives

Adjectives are used to describe more about the sense or meaning of a word or group of words so that our knowledge is more detailed.

The manager wanted action.

This rather bald statement tells us nothing about why the manager wanted action, nor does it tell us what kind of action he/she wanted. However, we could add some adjectives:

The angry(ADJECTIVE) manager wanted immediate (ADJECTIVE) action.

Although adjectives mostly come before the noun this is not always the case.

*On Fridays, the shopping mall is **busy**.*
*The overtime payment was **generous**.*

Although most people might think of adjectives as they appear in a phrase like 'a big man' ('big' being the adjective which tells us something about the man), they are sometimes formed from the past and present participles:

We could hear a humming sound.
She was saddened by the decayed landscape.

The above examples show how adjectives can describe nouns, but adjectives are also used for other purposes.

- to indicate possession:

  my desk, your telephone, his job, her company, its colour

- to ask questions:

  Which road did you take? What price would you put on this one?

- to indicate number or quantity:

    a few miles away, ten minutes later, half the time

- to single someone or something out:

    those machines, this word processor, that mechanic, these files

TASK 32 (L3)

Read the following passage carefully, and then go back over it and fill in the blanks with the appropriate words which will help to make the people and place sound good.

Harry Deane was a _____ man and his wife Marjory, was a _____ woman. They lived in a _____ house which had an _____ garden full of _____ flowers and _____ plants.

Now do the same exercise again, but this time fill in the blanks with words which will make the people and place sound unpleasant.

Conjunctions

Conjunctions are useful when two or more sentences which are short and closely connected to the same topic, can be added together. The main conjunctions are:

and, but, yet, so, or, next, then

Conjunctions can also be in pairs of words which appear in the same sentence, but always separated by other parts of the sentence.

not only . . . but also; either . . . or; neither . . . nor; both . . . and

For example:

He always arrived either very early, or terribly late.

TASK 33 (L3)

Read the following short sentences and join them together with conjunctions so that you form two or three longer ones.

Approach Manchester on the M56 continuing to the end of it.

The M56 becomes the A5106.

You come to another set of traffic lights.

Don't count the pedestrian ones.

Turn right into Barlow Moor Road.

You will be going in the direction of Didsbury.

Go past a filling station on your left.

When you reach another set of traffic lights, turn right.

Go along that road.

Turn first left.

Follow it until you see another set of lights.

The entrance to our block of flats is on the left just before them.

(See the suggested solution.)

Prepositions

The English language makes great use of prepositions, but the difficulty is that their correct use has to be learned because there are no rules to tell us when and where a particular preposition should be used.

The most commonly used prepositions are:

of, off, from, to, at, in, into, on, onto, over, under, through, up, over, down, before, after, near, by, beside

They are used as additions to verbs which change the meaning of the verb, giving it a particular meaning of its own:

to give　　*to transfer some benefit to someone without payment*

to give up　*to surrender, or resign*

Note the differences in meaning between the following pairs of verbs:

to throw and to throw down

to wash and to wash up

to pass and to pass over

to take and to take down

If you are ever in any doubt about which is the correct preposition to use with a verb, most good dictionaries have the information. The above examples were set only to draw your attention to the function of prepositions. However, the preposition is not always as close to the verb as it is in the examples above. A preposition often comes at the end of a sentence, especially in speech:

'You should have pushed the rubbish in the bins down, first.'

'Make sure you wash all the tables down.'

In writing, the formal rules of the language should be observed, so that a complex sentence with a dependent clause beginning with 'which' or 'who' should have the preposition in front of the pronoun.

The standard operating procedure is something with which you are no doubt familiar.

Verbs

These are the words we use for actions, or things that we do. For example:

to bake, to drive, to work, to swim, to sleep

Verbs are also used to describe mental processes such as:

to dream, to consider, to ponder, to wish, to idolize

If you think about it, you will notice that verbs change their form quite a lot, and this can cause confusion in English because the verbs are not always recognizable in their different forms. Before looking at an example of what that means, now is a good point to explain that the root form of verbs is usually written with a 'to' in front of it (e.g. 'to wish'). This is called the *infinitive*. Some verbs do not change very much at all from the infinitive form while others are almost unrecognizable.

The tenses

Verbs mostly change as a result of the tense we wish to express. The tense of the verb tells us something about the time period we are talking about, and there are three broad categories of time:

PAST   PRESENT   FUTURE

Just to complicate matters more, each of these tenses can be expressed in either a 'simple' or a 'continuous' form. If we look at a verb like 'to wish' we can see how it changes with the tense we want to express.

THE SIMPLE PRESENT	*I wish*
THE SIMPLE PAST	*I wished*
THE SIMPLE FUTURE	*I shall wish*
THE CONTINUOUS PRESENT	*I am wishing*
THE CONTINUOUS PAST	*I was wishing*
THE CONTINUOUS FUTURE	*I shall be wishing*

The person

The other consideration which can change the form of the verb is the person who is the subject of the verb, that is whether the verb is being used for I, he/she/it, we, you or they. If we return to the simple present form of the verb 'to wish' we shall see that it changes when 'I wish' becomes 'he/she/it wishes'. The words 'I, he, she, it, we, you and they' are called *pronouns* because they take the place of a noun, and they denote the person, as explained earlier in the chapter. They can be either singular or plural, and are set out as follows for ease of understanding:

PERSON	SINGULAR	PLURAL
1st	*I*	*We*
2nd	*You*	*You*
3rd	*He/she/it*	*They*

'You' is the same for both singular and plural because the original singular form 'thou' is no longer used, except in colloquial speech, and when depicting old-fashioned speech. This has given rise to the development of a new plural 'youse', which is also found only in colloquial speech, both in Britain and the USA. Its use is not recommended, especially in written English.

The voice

Sentences are formed differently in English, depending on whether we use the *active* or the *passive voice*. These are two ways of saying the same thing, but each places a different emphasis on what has happened. The following examples will illustrate the difference:

Example 1

Sam posted the letter. (ACTIVE)

Example 2

The letter was posted by Sam. (PASSIVE)

In Example 1 the emphasis is on the action carried out by Sam. He is the subject of the sentence and the verb (posted) describes what he did to the object of the sentence (the letter). In Example 2 the emphasis is on what happened to the letter, so 'the letter' becomes the subject, the verb (was posted), although still in the simple past tense, changes because it is in the passive voice, and the object is now 'Sam'.

The passive is often used to lessen the power of some statement, to make it sound less brutal, or to distance someone from an action. Consider the following sentences:

'Dad, I've lost my new watch.'

'Dad, my new watch has been lost.'

In the first sentence the onus is on you for being careless, whereas in the second sentence the concern shifts on to the fact that the watch has been lost.

In the passive, the past participle of the verb is always used, and it has to be helped by the verbs 'to have' or 'to be'.

Irregular verbs

Changes in verb endings, such as those described earlier in the chapter, are fairly easy to follow. It is obvious what the verb is. 'Wish', 'wishes', 'wished' or 'wishing' cannot really be mistaken for any other verb. In contrast, some verbs change completely so as to be almost unrecognizable in their different forms. Let us start with the infinitive form of the verb 'to be able (to)'.

THE SIMPLE PRESENT *I can*

THE SIMPLE PAST *I could*

THE SIMPLE FUTURE *I shall be able to*

Confusing though that may be, even more confusing is the fact that there is no continuous present form of the verb. If you want to prove this point, you will have noticed above that the continuous forms of verbs are usually formed by using 'I am' followed by the present participle, which ends in -ing, and if we say 'I am canning' it has nothing to do with being able to do something, it refers only to putting things into cans, so there is no continuous present. The continuous past is 'I used to be able'.

Another oddity among verbs is the verb 'to be' when it is used on its own, and not as an *auxiliary* verb (a verb which helps other verbs). In its simple tense forms it changes totally:

THE SIMPLE PRESENT *I am*

THE SIMPLE PAST *I was*

THE SIMPLE FUTURE *I shall be*

However, it is more regular in its continuous forms:

THE CONTINUOUS PRESENT *I am being*

THE CONTINUOUS PAST *I was being*

THE *(VERY RARE)* CONTINUOUS FUTURE *I shall be being*

Verbs like 'to wish', which follow a pattern, are called *regular* verbs, while those verbs like 'to be able to', which do not follow a pattern, are called *irregular* verbs.

You might well ask, 'What is the point of knowing about the different tenses, anyway. What possible good can it do me to know what they are?' One of the beauties of the English language is that you can be very precise about the way some action was done at a particular time. This is useful in all sorts of ways, whether in spoken or in written English. You are now aware that most regular verbs have a simple and a continuous form, which many other languages do not have, but do you understand what the difference is between those two forms?

TASK 34 (L2)

Just take a few moments to think about the difference between 'I work', and 'I am working'. If you are not able to put it into words immediately, make up a sentence for both forms and explain exactly what they mean in other words. (See the suggested solution.)

Summary of tenses

There are three forms of the verb which are used to make tenses in English:

THE INFINITIVE	*to walk*
THE PRESENT PARTICIPLE	*walking*
THE PAST PARTICIPLE	*walked*

Most verbs have both the simple and continuous forms in all tenses. Some verbs do not have a continuous form of the verb.

Regular verbs follow an observable pattern of changes according to which tense, person, or voice is being used. *Irregular* verbs often change to totally different words in the various tenses, which can lead to confusion.

So far, only three tenses have been identified, but there are more divisions than that (see table below). The examples used are all in the third person singular, using the regular verb 'to work'.

THE INFINITIVE	*to work*
PRESENT PARTICIPLE	*working*
PAST PARTICIPLE	*worked*

Tense	Form	Active	Passive
PRESENT	Simple	*works*	*is worked*
	Continuous	*is working*	*is being worked*
PAST	Simple	*worked*	*was worked*
	Continuous	*was working*	*was being worked*
PAST PERFECT	Simple	*has worked*	*has been worked*
	Continuous	*has been working*	
PLUPERFECT	Simple	*had worked*	*had been worked*
	Continuous	*had been working*	

(continued overleaf)

Tense	Form	Active	Passive
FUTURE	Simple	*will work*	*will be worked*
	Continuous	*will be working*	
FUTURE PERFECT	Simple	*will have worked*	*will have been worked*
	Continuous	*will have been working*	
CONDITIONAL PRESENT	Simple	*would work*	*would be worked*
	Continuous	*would be working*	
CONDITIONAL PERFECT	Simple	*would have worked*	*would have been worked*
	Continuous	*would have been working*	

Although most regular verbs change very little with the person being used, it is important to be sure that the subject and the verb agree. For example:

We were working very hard.

NOT

We was working very hard.

The use of 'we was' is not uncommon in some colloquial speech but must never be used in written form.

Another colloquial aberration which should not be used in written speech, is the use of the present simple tense instead of the simple past. For example:

We see him go into the house.

instead of

We saw him go into the house.

'Shall' 'will' 'should' or 'would'?

In everyday speech, the words 'shall' and 'will' are interchangeable, and as most of us use the contractions 'I'll' 'she'll' 'they'll' anyway, there is no way of saying which form is being used. It is a different matter in writing because contractions should never be used in formal writing, except when reporting direct speech. The same applies to 'should' and 'would', which are used in the contractions 'I'd' 'we'd' and 'they'd'.

'Shall' and 'will' express the future tense, and 'should' and 'would' express the future conditional tense.

'Shall' is used with the first person singular and plural, thus:

I shall be in the office tomorrow.
We shall be at the exhibition.

The second and third persons use 'will' :

You will hear from us in a few days.
She will take you there herself.

But, when 'shall' and 'will' are reversed, it introduces a sense of command or determination:

You shall follow my orders.
I will succeed.

Similarly, in the future conditional:

I should like to see it.
We should have a new car.

but:

You would be happier.
He would be better off.

Where you want to express determination, you say:

I would do it if there were time.

Compare that with the use of 'should' in the second and third persons:

You should thank her for the gift.
He should try to help his friends.

As you will see, this use of 'should' introduces a sense of obligation, and can be replaced with 'ought' without changing the meaning.

There is also some confusion in people's minds about when to use 'could' and when to use 'would/should'. This is easy to sort out when you are aware that they come from different verbs: 'would/should' and 'will' are the future conditional and the future form of all verbs; 'could' and 'can' are the past and present tense of 'to be able'. There is therefore a big difference between:

I should be pleased if you would do the job.

which means that you are being given the choice about whether or not to do the job, and:

I should be pleased if you could do the job.

which means that I do not know if you are able to do the job or not, but hope that you can.

The use of participles

Another difficulty in written form involves the use of participles. You may remember that there are two forms: the present participle, which ends in -ing (e.g. working) and the past participle, which usually ends in -ed (e.g. added). You may also remember that they can both be used as adjectives:

a working museum
added value

Both forms of the participle can also be used as nouns, the present participle being known as a *gerund*:

Her thinking was crystal clear.
The initiated do not have to attend.

Both the present and the past participles can be used to form clauses, which have the function of an adjective. But you must be sure that the word which immediately follows such clauses is the pronoun being described. Look at the following two examples:

Example 1
Thinking about her colleague's remark, she went to see her manager immediately.

Example 2
Having crashed into the empty car, he drove off at high speed.

The first clause of Example 1 up to the comma, tells us something about why she should go and see her manager, while in the second sentence, we know why he drove off at high speed. In each of the examples above, the clause which is called a *participial construction* (horrible name!) is related to the pronoun immediately following it. But it pays to take care when using present and past participles in this way because there is a danger that you could end up with some very strange meanings.

TASK 35 (L2/3)

Look at the examples which follow and write down what they mean, grammatically. Then rewrite the sentence, grammatically, to show what the writer really intended to say.

1 Running from the car, his suit got soaking wet.

2 Having dug in the field all day, the hole collected a lot of water.

3 Waving a flag from the hilltop, the enemy advanced by mistake.

4 Having landed a big order, the commission was enormous.

(See the suggested solution.)

Adverbs

In the same way that nouns are qualified by adjectives, verbs can be extended by adverbs. Verbs are qualified or altered by adverbs, or adverbial phrases. Phrases are different from sentences because they contain neither a subject nor a finite verb, and those which perform the same function as an adverb are called adverbial phrases.

Adverbs or adverbial phrases also give more detail about questions of:

- when something happened;
- where something happened;
- why something happened;
- how something happened.

SUBJECT	VERB	OBJECT	ADVERBIAL PHRASE
He	*received*	*the result*	*on his birthday.*

Look at the following simple sentence:

William (NOUN) swims (FINITE VERB).

It tells us nothing about how the subject (William) swims. But additional information could be added using an adverb:

William swims quickly.

Alternatively, we could have used 'slowly', 'determinedly', 'purposefully', 'enthusiastically'. Or:

William swims for dear life.
William swims without conviction.
William swims around in circles.

The adverb can be a word which usually ends in -ly. For example:

poorly, subtly, efficiently, quickly, lightly, terribly
The new accounts clerk performed badly.

Note also that when verb extensions are not single words but phrases, they need not follow the verb:

SUBJECT	VERB	VERB EXTENSION
He	*was asleep*	*by the last stroke of midnight from the town clock.*

That sentence could also be written:

By the last stroke of midnight from the town clock he was asleep.

Another point to remember is that not all adverbs end in -ly; a few words which perform the same function as an adverb do not:

well, better, fast, low

Sometimes an adverb can be used to modify another adverb, as in:

It was obvious that he was running extremely fast.

Although the word 'fast' acts as an adverb to the verb 'was running', 'extremely', which comes after the verb 'was running', modifies the second adverb 'fast', which in turn tells us something about how he was running.

A proper sentence

Even in the most prestigious of journals you can come across what grammarians call the 'incomplete sentence', which looks something like this:

> **And water, there in the fields, cold, dark and forbidding.**

It is not a grammatically correct sentence because it does not have the necessary, basic elements. It must contain:

1 a subject, and
2 a finite verb.

There must be a subject, even if it contains the kind of construction where the subject is not written or said, but it is understood. For example:

> **(You) Get out!**

As has already been pointed out, the verb must agree with the number and person, and it must be in a tense form. When a verb satisfies all three requirements, it is said to be a finite verb. The sentence used as an example above, has no verb in it.

Constructing more complex sentences

The analysis of sentence structure is called *syntax* and you have already had a look at some useful information which will help you to tackle this task. The object of doing so is to help you to write fault-free English which communicates your meaning to others clearly.

As you already know a sentence has a subject and a finite verb.

SUBJECT	FINITE VERB
I	*work.*

Sometimes it also has a subject, a finite verb and an object.

SUBJECT	FINITE VERB	OBJECT
I	*cooked*	*a meal.*

It can also have a subject, a finite verb, an indirect object and a direct object.

SUBJECT	FINITE VERB	INDIRECT OBJECT	DIRECT OBJECT
I	*cooked*	*(for) my wife*	*a meal.*

TASK 36 (L2)

Look at the following three sentences and pick out:

a the subject,

b the verb, and

c the object in each case.

1 Arthur tried to find a job.

2 The blazing aircraft was abandoned by the injured pilot.

3 Tired and unhappy, the weary traveller eventually crawled into a dry barn.

(See the suggested solution.)

Spelling

Put at its simplest, English spelling is difficult because English words are pronounced in a way which bears no relation to how they are spelt. There are several good reasons for this, the most important being that, as mentioned earlier, English has about forty-nine recognizable sounds, but only twenty-six letters in the alphabet!

'How are the others made up?' you might well ask. The answer is a mixture of diphthongs and combinations of letters, together with several random pronunciations of the same combination of letters. Take the pronunciation of 'ough', for example:

cough as in 'off'
rough as in 'puff'
though as in 'low'
plough as in 'now'
through as in 'true'
thought as in 'claw'.

The above example serves to warn us not to place any dependence on the pronunciation of a word as a means of helping us to spell it. Some of the sounds represented by 'ough' are also represented by other combinations of letters in other words. Yet another problem is caused by regional differences in pronunciation, and changes to pronunciation over time.

The original languages of the United Kingdom were Celtic: Welsh, Scots, Irish and Cornish. Although they have largely died out as first languages, their influence is carried on into the words which have been absorbed into English. Spelling is also influenced by other languages such as French, German, Scandinavian, Greek and Latin. You would have to be extremely clever to have a widespread knowledge of all of these, but understanding how each one might affect some words will help you to remember how the words of that origin are spelt.

Plurals

The simplest plural form in English is to add an 's' to the singular:

pencil → pencils, telephone → telephones, chair → chairs, day → days

There is a slight complication when a singular ends in 'sh', 'ch', 'ss', 's', 'x' and 'z'. The plural 'es' is added then:

dish → dishes, pitch → pitches, grass → grasses, box → boxes

Yet another plural ending is found in words ending in a 'y'. The 'y' changes to 'ies' in the plural:

company → companies, lorry → lorries

But when the final 'y' follows a vowel, that rule does not apply:

day → days, bay → bays

The first difficult plurals are such common words that we hardly notice how peculiar they are:

man → men, child → children

Very few of such plural endings still exist in modern English. Their origin is German (Saxon or Old English).

TASK 37 (L2)

Change the words in **bold** in the following passage into plurals:

The little fishing **boat** sailed into the **bay** with a **cargo** of **fish** and the people all cheered heartily as **it was** unloaded onto the **quayside**. The **crew was** ecstatic at their reception and, as soon as the fish had been sold, made their way to the little **inn**. It was not long before **a sailor** got into a fight and **was** chased away by the tough **man** of the **town**.

(See the suggested solution.)

While we are on the subject of imported foreign words, Latin and French have a lot to answer for! For example:

bureau → bureaux, radius → radii, formula → formulae

There are also a number of plurals which are difficult to explain, other than by their origins. The German/Scandinavian word 'mouse' becomes 'mice' in the plural but the French word 'mousse' becomes 'mousses'.

Other words which do not seem to follow the rules, a fairly common occurrence in English unfortunately, are:

tomato → tomatoes, potato → potatoes, money → monies, sheep → sheep, fish → fish (sometimes fishes)

and a host of others which leave you with no other alternative but to learn them as you come across them.

There is a group of words which cannot make up their mind about what their plural really is – words which end in 'f' in the singular. Note:

loaf → loaves, shelf → shelves, wolf → wolves; reef → reefs

Prefixes

Prefixes are simply added to the front of an existing word in order to change its meaning. They are mostly Latin and Greek, but there are some which come from Germanic languages and are easier for us to understand. The following list of prefixes will help you to understand the meanings of unfamiliar words, and will also help your spelling. The meanings of the prefixes are not exact but indications only. Examples are given in order to help you understand the meanings.

Prefix	Meaning (approx.)	Example
a-, an-	no, not	*amoral, anarchy*
ab-	from	*abstract, abstain*
a-, ac-, ad-	to, added to	*application, accessory*
ambi-	of both kinds	*ambidextrous*
ante-	before	*antenatal*
anti-	against	*antipathy, antiperspirant*
arch-	superior	*archbishop, arch-enemy*
auto-	self	*automatic, autobiography*
bene-	well	*benefit, benevolent*
bi-	two	*binoculars, binary*
circum-	around	*circumference, circumvent*
co-, com-, con-	with others	*co-operate, combine, connect*
contra-	against	*contradict*
de-	down, away	*descend, destroy*
di-	two	*dialogue, dissect*
dis-	negative	*disappear*
e-, ex-	out of	*exit, evolve, expel*
geo-	earth	*geometry*
in-	into	*insert, instil*
im-, in-, ir-	not	*improper, innumerable, irregular, also illegal*
intra-, intro-	within	*intravenous, introduce*
mal-	ill, bad	*malady, malevolence*
mis-	not, wrongly	*misspell, mistake, mishandle*
mono-	one, single	*monarch, monotonous*
non-, not-	not	*nonsense, non-toxic, nothing*
ob-, oc-	in the way of	*obstruct, occult*
per-	through, by, all	*perforate, percentage, perfect*
phil-	liking	*philanthropist, philately*
photo-	of light	*photocopy, photograph*
poly-	many	*polytechnic, polygon*
post-	after	*postpone, post-war*
pre-	before	*precede*
pro-	for	*proactive, pro-European*
psycho-	of the mind	*psychology, psychopath*
re-	again, back	*repeat, revenge*

(continued overleaf)

Prefix	Meaning (approx.)	Example
se-	apart, without	*seclude, secure*
semi-	half	*semicircle, semi-skilled*
sub-	under, lower	*submerge, subservient*
super-	over, above	*superhuman, supervisor*
tele-	far	*telephone, telescope*
theo-	of gods	*theology*
trans-	across	*transport, transcript*
tri-	of three	*tripod, triangle*
un-	not	*unknown, unlock*
uni-	of one	*union, unilateral*

If your vocabulary is in need of being extended, it is a good idea to keep a notebook with you at all times so that you can make a note of any new words you come across. Always make the effort to look up the meaning, or meanings, in the dictionary at the earliest opportunity, and commit the correct spelling to memory at the same time.

There are few difficulties in the spelling of prefixes.

'Arch-' is given the pronunciation you would expect, the 'ch' being soft as in 'cherry'. Beware other words such as 'architect' where the 'ch' has a hard sound, as in 'choir'. This is because it does not have the 'arch-' prefix, but comes from a different origin.

Words with the prefix 'bene-' are often misspelt because of the tendency of English speakers to give most vowels the same sound, especially second vowels: 'predetermine' sounds like prediatermine.

Now say the following words out loud, paying attention to the vowels which are in underlined. Notice their similar sounds.

sender, below, preparation, principal, editor, monotonous

The prefix 'phil-' has the combination 'ph' which is pronounced like 'f' in 'fish', and it never varies from that.

The last one 'psycho-' has the unfortunate silent first 'p', the 'y' sounds like the 'y' in 'sky', and the 'ch' has a hard sound like 'choir'.

TASK 38 (L3)

Rewrite the following passage changing the words in **bold** for other words which have prefixes according to the key at the end of it.

*Toby Grimes was a wealthy man who, at the early age of forty one, had managed to **(1) gather together** a large fortune. He lived quietly in a small village in rural Oxfordshire where few people knew how wealthy he really was because he did not **(2) talk** to many of the residents.*

*His wealth came from **(3) various** sources including banking, shipping, mining and chemical manufacturing. One of his chemical plants was situated in a poor African country where safety standards were not high and, although its presence brought prosperity to the locals, they hated it for its accident rate and the **(4) bad smell** which hung over the area permanently. Some of the locals had tried to take him to court many times but the prosperity which the plant brought gave Toby some influence with the military dictatorship which **(5) stopped** the locals from bringing a successful legal action against him.*

*Those who knew nothing of his money-making activities admired the quiet Oxfordshire man who **(6) claimed** to be a nature lover. Their admiration was to be dashed when news of his links with a military dictator appeared in the newspapers. The activities of opposition groups had increased to the extent that they had partially destroyed the chemical plant in their attempts to **(7) undermine** the dictator's regime.*

Each word in bold in the passage has a number before it and the key which follows has a prefix with each number. Your task is to find an alternative word with the correct prefix and the same meaning as the word in bold which has the corresponding number in the passage.

   (1) ac-   (2) com-   (3) di-   (4) mal-   (5) pre-   (6) pro-   (7) sub-

(See the suggested solution.)

Suffixes

Suffixes are added to the ends of words, and also change their meanings. The difference between prefixes and suffixes, apart from being at opposite ends of the word, is that the prefix does not usually change the word to form another part of speech whereas the suffix often does:

circle (NOUN), add a prefix → semicircle (NOUN), but

impose (VERB), add a suffix → imposition (NOUN)

By being aware of the various suffixes and what parts of speech they belong to, you will be able to treat the word correctly in a grammatical sense in written work. It will also help you to extend your vocabulary by enabling you to construct suitable words from base words, to fit in with what you want to express. To help you in this task there is a list of suffixes below, with a note on how they are used, together with an example.

Suffix	Use	Examples
-able	To make adjectives with the meaning of 'able to be'	*portable*
-an, -ant	Makes a noun or an adjective meaning 'a thing or person is'	*attendant*
-er, -or	Added to a base word to give a sense of 'a person who, or animal that does'	*driver, pointer*
-ery	forming nouns to denote a class of things, people or animals	*greenery, machinery, piggery*
-ic, -ique	used to form adjectives and nouns from a base word	*Arabic, alcoholic, poetic, mechanic*
-ise	forms nouns of quality, state or function	*exercise, expertise, merchandise*
-ish	used to form adjectives, nature of, or somewhat	*British, childish, reddish*
-ism	used to form abstract nouns of action, conduct or belonging	*baptism, heroism, Americanism*
-ist	used to form personal nouns of 'one who is'	*antagonist, fatalist, cyclist, pianist*
-ition	used to form nouns from verbs	*television.*
-ious	forms adjectives with the sense of 'characterized by, full of'	*invidious, spacious, religious, curious.*
-ity	forms nouns denoting quality or condition of something/someone	*authority, humility, humidity, porosity*
-ly	forms adjectives from nouns with 'quality of', and adverbs from adjectives	*motherly, daily, nastily, volubly*
-logy	forms nouns denoting character of speech, area of study or discourse	*tautology, biology, trilogy.*
-oid	forms adjectives and nouns with the sense of resembling a form	*asteroid, humanoid, cuboid*

As for the spelling and pronunciation of suffixes, it is as well to note that the first one on the list '-able' sometimes sounds like 'ible' but you should not confuse the two spellings. If the word means 'able to be' then it will be spelt '-able'.

Difficulties can occur with the two suffixes '-ition' , which sounds like 'shun' or 'shon', and '-ious', which sounds like 'shus'. The 'shun' sound can also be made by the suffixes '-sion' '-ssion' which have the same function as '-ition', by far the most used. The only thing is to learn the 'shun' words which end in something other than '-ition'. Words ending in the 'shus' sound may also have alternative spellings, which are '-scious', '-tious' or '-cious'.

A word which ends in 'y' usually changes it to 'i' with the addition of a suffix:

friendly → friendliness

When '-ly' is added to a word which ends in 'l' that final 'l' is usually retained:

fundamental → fundamentally

If a suffix beginning with a vowel is added to a base word ending in 'e', the 'e' is usually dropped:

fragile → fragility

As is to be expected in English, there are some exceptions. Where the suffix '-able' is added to a word ending in 'e', the 'e' is sometimes kept. If you are not sure, look in your dictionary.

In addition to the above spelling traps, there are a number of words which change with a vengeance when they move into different forms. There is no rule to guide you except to say, write them down when you find them and refer to your notebook from time to time in order to refresh your memory. Some examples of the kind of erratic changes which are to be found in English are listed below :

to maintain (VERB) → maintenance (NOUN)

humour (NOUN) → humorous (ADJ)

to benefit (VERB) → beneficial (ADJ)

brief (ADJ) → brevity (NOUN)

Vowels and consonants

The vowels A E I O U can help you to spell words correctly, but you have to pay attention to the way the word is pronounced. The old rule that I comes before E except after C may not always follow, but it nearly always does:

grievance, deceive, thief

but

neither, neighbour, reign

A short vowel is usually an indication that it is going to be followed by a double consonant:

litter, spinner, bidder, putter

By contrast, long vowels followed by a consonant usually have an 'e' after them:

site, finite, bite, fire, jibe, tribe, alive

The most common *double* vowels in English are OO and EE:

look, book, soon, feel, reel

Note that when a prefix is added which doubles the vowel, they are sounded separately:

pre-eminent, cooperate, coordinate

Words ending in 'y' usually change to an 'i' when the word is made longer:

lonely → loneliness, happy → happier

Consonants are the letters which are not vowels and here are a few tips which might help you to spell a word correctly when you are unsure.

Single syllable words with a vowel coming before the single consonant at the end of the word double that consonant when a suffix is added:

big → biggest, fit → fitter, dig → digger

Words where the final consonant is followed by an 'e' drop the 'e' after the addition of a suffix:

dive → diving, live → living, game → gaming

However, as always, beware the exceptions – 'age' can be either 'ageing' or 'aging'.

The suffix '-ly' is added to all base words with the exception of 'dull' which becomes 'dully'. (Note that 'duly' is the adverb of 'due'.)

A complication with consonants is that there are a large number of words in English which have silent consonants. Those consonants are:

g   h   k   p   w

For example:

gnaw, hour, knife, pseudonym, write

A sound which appears often in English is the 'sh' sound. Apart from the 'sh' combination, it is represented in numerous other ways, as the following short list of words demonstrates:

fiction, anxious, precious, complexion, conscience, attaché

Be aware of them and remember in which words they appear.

Words which sound the same

This section began by pointing out one spelling combination which has a number of different pronunciations. It is fitting that it ends with a warning about the reverse situation, that there are a lot of words which sound the same, but have a completely different spelling and meaning. The technical name for such words is the rather frightening 'homophones' which simply means 'words which sound the same'. The list which follows does not contain every one in the language, but it does contain the ones you are most likely to meet. Memorize the various spellings and the meanings so that you will be in no doubt about them when you are writing.

air / heir
aisle / isle
anti / ante
arc / ark
ascent / assent
ate / eight
aye / eye
bale / bail
ban / bann
bare / bear
baron / barren
beech / beach
been / bean
born / borne
bough / bow
bury / berry
ceiling / sealing
cereal / serial
choir / quire
chord / cord
complement / compliment
council / counsel
course / coarse
cue / queue
dear / deer
deuce / juice
die / dye
draft / draught
due / dew
fair / fare
fate / fete
feet / feat
fiancé / fiancée
find / fined
for / fore / four
forward / foreword
foul / fowl
frieze / freeze
fur / fir
gage / gauge
gait / gate

great / grate
guerilla / gorilla
hare / hair
heel / heal
hoarse / horse
hold / holed
hole / whole
hour / our
lain / lane
leased / least
led / lead
lightning / lightening
load / lode
loan / lone
made / maid
manner / manor
meat / mete / meet
might / mite
mind / mined
morn / mourn
nave / knave
need / knead
new / knew
night / knight
nit / knit
no / know
not / knot
oh / owe
or / ore
quay / key
pain / pane
pair / pear
palate / palette
pale / pail
peel / peal
peer / pier
plane / plain
pleas / please
poor / pour
principle / principal
put / putt

rain / reign / rein
real / reel
review / revue
roll / role
root / route
sale / sail
scene / seen
scent / sent
seam / seem
see / sea
shake / sheikh
shore / sure
sight / cite / site
soul / sole
sow / so / sew
stationary / statio
steel / steal
straight / strait
swayed / suede
sweet / suite
tail / tale
taught / taut
tee / tea
their / there / they
thrown / throne
tide / tied
time / thyme
to / two / too
urn / earn
vale / veil
wait / weight
way / weigh / whe
weather / whethe
weir / we're
what / watt
where / wear / wa
won / one
you / yew / ewe
your / yore / yaw

Depending on where you come from, the examples in the above list of homophones may or may not make much sense. Most Scots will find it hard to believe that anyone could confuse 'where' and 'wear', but in the north-west of England some people confuse 'are' and 'our', or 'we're', 'were' and 'where'. Unfortunately it is impossible to include all the individual differences of local accents; you will have to be aware of them and make a note of any that come to light.

Using a dictionary

Everyone who is involved with reading or writing, whether at school, college, university or work, should possess and be able to use a dictionary. The reason why is quite simple. Unless you have a very good memory indeed, you will not be able to remember every word which you are ever likely to want to use or read. Everyone's personal vocabulary differs to some extent from everyone else's because the words which one person knows and uses are not always the same as another's, so the words which we encounter through other people will sometimes be unfamiliar to us.

Each person's vocabulary can best be understood in terms of someone standing in the middle of a flat landscape. The *foreground* is familiar to us and it is easy for us to explain all the small differences in it. The *middle ground* is still reasonably well known to us but we cannot see, and cannot be sure that we understand all the little differences in it. Last of all, there is the *far distance*, where almost everything is unfamiliar and incapable of explanation without referring to another source of information. As far as vocabulary is concerned, a dictionary is probably the most important source book for this purpose, so let us start by looking up the dictionary definition of 'dictionary'. The following one is from the *Concise Oxford Dictionary*:

> di'ctionary n. Book explaining, usu, in alphabetical order, the words of a language or words and topics of some special subject, author, etc., wordbook, lexicon (French-English, etc. —, list of French etc. words with English etc. translation or explanation; dictionary of Americanisms, of architecture, of the Bible, of proverbs, Dictionary of National Biography, Shakespeare dictionary, etc.)[f. med. L *dictionarium* (manuale manual) & *dictionarius* (liber book) f. L dictio (see prec, -ARY')]

You will be able to understand most of the above, but there are bound to be parts of the entry which appear strange and definitely unfamiliar. There is a great deal of information included in dictionary entries most of which is explained at the beginning of the book. To make it easier for you, the following brief guide is given.

1   *Accepted spelling(s)* are given against each entry: organize, -ise

2   *Pronunciation.* A phonetic equivalent alphabet is given at the front of the book which is used to show the accepted pronunciation when it differs from the spelling: heir (ar), loser (looz-). Vowels have the symbol ˘ above them to show that they are short vowels and ¯ above them indicates long vowels. The stress on a syllable is indicated by the symbol ' which comes immediately after the stressed one.

3   *Parts of speech.* The abbreviation which immediately follows the entry tells us which part of speech the word may be used as: n = noun, v = verb, a = adjective, adv = adverb, etc.

4   *Colloquial words.* This means that the word is used in an informal way: horre'ndous a. (colloq). Colloquial words should not be used in formal writing so, if you are not sure, check in the dictionary.

5   *Plurals.* These are formed by the addition of 's' or 'es' in English and are only mentioned where the plural is formed differently: die n (pl dice, also colloq. as sing.) Sometimes there are two plurals, either of which is acceptable: octopus n. (pl. —es, or octopodes pr —opodez)

6   *Meanings.* Some words have more than one meaning: faint a. timid, dim or faint v.i. & n. lose consciousness, lose courage, give way. The different meanings are usually listed separately.

7   *Compound words* are where one word is linked to another in order to form a new word: green-eyed, plunge-bath. These are listed under the basic word entry, the compounds being indicated thus: —eyed. The symbol — indicates the basic word.

8   *Etymology.* This means the origin(s) of the word entry, the language or languages from which it originated. The list of etymological abbreviations is usually listed at the front of the book, e.g.: F French, Gk Greek, L Latin, ME Middle English.

9   *Other information.* A useful addition to dictionaries is the list of abbreviations in common use: ACAS, AA, RAC. Some dictionaries have them in the main body of the book. You may also find the following:

- The Greek and Russian alphabets, together with pronunciation guide.
- British, American and Metric weights and measures equivalents.
- The principal monetary units of the world.

TASK 39 (L2/3)

Look up the following words in a good dictionary and note down what part of speech each one is (verb, noun etc.), whether it has an alternative spelling and the etymology of each one.

collagen   depoliticize   gripe   nemesis   sally

(See the suggested solution.)

Punctuation

Beginning and ending

By now you should be aware of what a sentence is, and how it can be joined to others to make up complex sentences. This can now be recognized by you grammatically, but there is another way in which the beginnings and endings are indicated. Sentences always start by putting a capital letter at the beginning of the first word, and they are ended by putting a full stop (or *period*) at the end.

The only other occasions when capitals are used are:

- when a word is a proper noun:
  London   the Thames   John Major   Ford Motor Company

- when a name is abbreviated to initials:
  the BBC   ICI

  The same applies to educational qualifications, like BA or MA, and to honours and decorations, like DFC and KCB.

In normal business communications, the full stop is sometimes used at the end of standard expressions which are not true sentences:

Stop here.   No entry.   Keep out.   Danger.   High voltage.

and many others besides.

To return for a moment to abbreviations, the full stop is sometimes used to separate the letters of them, even when the letters are what is known as 'lower case':

etc. enc. viz. c.c.

It should be said that many such abbreviations in letters, memos and reports are no longer typed with the full stops. This applies particularly to business letters where the address, date and references are all typed without the use of full stops.

The exclamation mark

Occasionally you will encounter an exclamation mark at the end of a group of words:

Mind your head!   Halt!

or even:

Westward Ho!
(the only English place name to end in an exclamation mark)

It should be noted that the exclamation mark takes the place of the full stop; no full stop should be added after it. The need to use an exclamation mark in business correspondence, or other communication will not occur frequently. Its main use is to show shock, excitement, sarcasm and other strongly felt emotions.

I was pleased to note that our order arrived two days early!

Question mark

Another way of ending a sentence is by the use of a question mark. Of course, it will be used only when a direct question has been asked:

Are you seriously asking for a price increase of 20%?

In reported speech there is no need to use the question mark:

I understand that our buyer asked you if you seriously intended to increase your prices by 20%, and we would like an answer soon.

The colon and the semicolon

Both of these punctuation marks do not exactly finish sentences in the way which has been referred to in the first part of this section, but in effect they do. As you will have seen in the section on complex sentence structure, a complex sentence is often no more than two or more sentences welded together by one of several grammatical devices. Both the colon and the semicolon are two ways of achieving this effect.

Several hundreds of years ago, the colon was used to break up what were long sentences. It had the effect of balancing the sentence in the middle, like the old style of scales, by creating a longer pause than you would expect from a comma. The use to which the colon is put nowadays is as a way of introducing a list.

The maintenance engineers' overtime rota is as follows: J Watson, F Dunn, A Morris.

The previous example is the format most used with the colon, but it is still acceptable to use it in the middle of a sentence for the purpose of breaking up the sentence.

The use of the semicolon seems to present people with even more problems than the colon, and its widespread misuse is ample illustration of this fact. It tends to be used to make lists in the way that should be reserved for the comma. Its real usefulness is in placing the emphasis or importance of a sentence with two clauses, on the last clause. The clauses must be closely connected to the same theme for this to work. Consider the following two sentences:

Last year productivity per employee went up by 20%. This means that wage increases will go up by 10% in the current year.

Because the information in the two sentences is closely connected, it would be better to write them in the following way:

> *Last year productivity per employee went up by 20%; this means that wage increases will go up by 10% in the current year.*

The second version leaves the reader in no doubt about the connection between the two sentences. Here are two more examples to show how effective this device can be:

> *The train arrived at last; everyone was so relieved that they cheered spontaneously.*
>
> *You have two choices; either you accept the new terms, or you look for alternative employment.*

The comma

Just like the full stops which were mentioned above, the comma appears far less frequently than it used to in normal business correspondence. Here is an example of how addresses used to be typed on letterheads thirty to forty years ago:

> *Messrs., J. & P. White & Co., Ltd.,*
>
> *151, Marsh Lane,*
>
> *Cambridge,*
>
> *Cambs.*

The typing of the date fared no better:

> *25th., April, 1952.*

They certainly liked their dots and commas in those days!

At the present time you will be unlikely to find commas in some pieces of text, whether it be in books, in letters, or in reports. The question is, where have all the commas gone? Quite clearly many of the commas which festooned our pages many years ago were quite superfluous. They added nothing to our understanding of the written text, so you must be wondering when they ought to be used and what function they serve.

Commas mean meaning

Sometimes the comma is essential to give the correct meaning to a piece of writing. Consider the following:

I went to meet my brother, the sailor, at four o'clock.

I went to meet my brother the sailor at four o'clock.

In the first instance there is a suggestion that I have more than one brother, while in the second I am simply saying that my brother is a sailor.

Making lists

When a letter or a report mentions things one after the other commas are used to separate them. These might be qualities:

The new offices were spacious, comfortable, well appointed and had ample car parking space.

Or they might be goods to be ordered:

The contracts manager urgently requested the stores department to make available two tonnes of timber, three loads of external bricks, five pallets of plasterboard and forty litres of paint.

In both cases each item listed is separated by a comma, except for the last one, which is preceded by 'and', and has no need for a comma before it.

A pause or a breather?

The idea of a breathing space in written language is only psychological, but it seems to make a difference to the way that we read and absorb written material. This is a good guide to use when you are writing something, ask yourself if you would take a breath anywhere in the text if you were to speak it. Note the difference when commas are inserted into the passage below.

There is every reason to think that two extra staff would be of great benefit to the department but those benefits have to be weighed against the extra cost and Alison has a budget to keep to.

There is every reason to think that two extra staff would be of great benefit to the department, but those extra benefits have to be weighed against the extra cost, and Alison has a budget to keep to.

In no way do the two commas alter the sense of the passage, but they somehow make its sense easier to absorb. Note also that there is a comma before the part of it which begins, 'and Alison . . .'. In this case the 'and' does not signal the last item on a list, but the development of an argument where a pause aids its understanding.

Putting secondary ideas or information into parenthesis

Sometimes we want to draw attention to an idea, or additional information which might be useful to the reader, although it may not be essential, and it would not affect the grammar of the sentence if it were to be removed.

> **The application form and supporting documents are then sent to the Actuarial Department, where a final check is made on the premium, and the staff there send the policy to the insured.**

The part between the commas, 'where a final check is made on the premium' is information which is secondary to the main information, and it can be removed without affecting the grammar.

To be, or not to be a comma

If you are torn between putting a comma or a full stop in the passage you are writing, think about two important aspects first.

1   Will the sentence be too long if you use a comma?
2   Will the part you write after the comma contain an idea which can stand on its own?

If the answer to either, or both, is a 'yes', then you should put a full stop and start another sentence for the separate idea.

Inverted commas

These are used mostly when writing reported speech, that is, writing down exactly what someone has said. It is normal nowadays to use single inverted commas, although in some older books you will find double inverted commas used for this purpose.

> *The tall, tanned ski instructor turned to the girl in the red and white suit and said, 'Julia, what are your plans for this evening?' Julia went slightly red as she replied, 'Your friend André has asked me to a party.'*

As you can see, everything about the reported speech is within the inverted commas, including the question mark. The same would have applied to an exclamation mark.

Quotation marks are normally double inverted commas, and they certainly must be so if the quotation is part of reported speech, otherwise there is some confusion about what is, and is not, being said:

> *'The MD made it clear in his address by pointing out that "This practice has got to stop" when he was talking about the overtime people did.'*

The apostrophe

For some reason the apostrophe gives people a lot of problems, and this in turn gives problems to the reader, not to mention annoyance that the writer does not know how to use them!

One of the problems is, that even when people do not know how to use apostrophes properly, they still insist on putting them in their writing. The uses of apostrophes are as follows:

1 To show that a person or thing belongs to another person or thing.

2 To show that something has been left out.

Ownership or possession

We do not say:

> *the office of the company*
>
> *the room of men*
>
> *the pen of Jennifer*

It is more usual to say:

> *the company's office*

> *the men's cloakroom*
>
> *Jennifer's pen*

The rule is simple: to show ownership, put an apostrophe after the word which possesses and add an 's'. Where the word is a plural ending in 's', the final 's' is omitted. For example:

> *the worker's breaks*   *(the breaks of one worker)*
>
> *the workers' breaks*   *(the breaks of more than one worker)*

If, however, the noun is in the singular and ends in 's' you have the choice of either adding the apostrophe plus the 's', or the apostrophe only:

> *James' lunch*

or

> *Thomas's chair, the glass's rim*

That seems perfectly straightforward, except that there are a number of words in English which already express possession without the need to add an apostrophe. A few of those words are as follows:

> *The bill showed £20 as **its** total.*
>
> ***Yours** is the chair by the window.*
>
> *The waste land next door is **ours**.*
>
> ***His** car is dark red and **hers** is white.*

So remember the following:

> *employee's = belonging to one employee*
>
> *employees' = belonging to more than one employee*
>
> *employees = the plural, i.e. more than one employee*

When something is left out

Instead of saying 'I am', 'he is', 'we are', 'they are', etc., we say and write:

> *I'm   he's   we're   they're*

From the examples above we can see which letters have been missed out of what are sometimes known as 'contractions'. Note, however, that in normal business communications with external organizations, contractions are not to be used.

Other contractions which are often used are:

don't = do not

hadn't = had not

wouldn't = would not

Be aware of:

won't = will not

can't = cannot (one word, not 'can not')

it's = 'it is' or 'it has' ('its' is a possessive word)

If you remember the rules of how to express what you want to say, there should be no problem with getting the form right.

The hyphen, the dash and brackets

The function of the hyphen is to link two words together because, when they are linked in this way, they actually form one word. Less frequently, more than one word is linked in this way, and when it is it is often done for humorous effect, but not always. The reason for this device is that there is probably no single, equivalent word which expresses the same meaning as well:

right-handed	*left-handed*	*well-meaning*
full-bodied	*up-and-over*	*up-and-coming*

As well as joining two words into one word, the hyphen can be used to indicate that a word has been split into two parts at the end of a line, particularly in letters which are typewritten. This is not as common nowadays as it used to be, because of the use of word processors which can justify margins without resorting to splitting words.

Looking at the current sales figures we have reached the conclusion that it is no longer a viable proposition.

Note that the hyphen appears at the right-hand end of the line only; it is not necessary to put a hyphen at the left-hand end of the next line.

In formal business correspondence the use of the dash should be discouraged. It has the reputation of being a lazy person's method of punctuation. It does have its uses, however. It can best be used as a way of adding an afterthought to a letter or memo, but should not appear in a well thought-out report.

> *The best way to get to the motorway is to turn left out of our road, follow that road for about half a mile, then turn right down King's Avenue. Go to the end where there is a 'T' junction, turn right and go straight on until you reach the motorway – and don't forget to fill up before you go on to the motorway!*

Another use is to insert information in the middle of a passage, with a dash at the beginning and a dash at the end of it, in much the same way as you might do with commas. This piece is put into parenthesis and as such, does not affect the grammar of the original sentence.

> *When winding an armature – even using the new machinery – make sure that the wire is absolutely tight.*

The function of putting things in parenthesis is sometimes carried out by inserting information between brackets, but the effect is the same.

> *The result of the trials (see Appendix 4) shows that there is a clear case for introducing more robust brake pads.*

TASK 40 (L3)

Read the passage below carefully before rewriting it with the correct punctuation:

> *the day the sun disappeared can you imagine anything as frightening as having to live without the sun well that was precisely what happened to a small community on a small pacific isle one hundred and fifty years ago this week when jaime martinez and his family had been living on the island for about ten years and all of their children had been born there jaime and his wife conchita had moved there with the help of a wealthier brother in order to avoid religious retribution all that time they had enjoyed a good but simple life in what had seemed to them heaven on earth but in the words of the old proverb all good things come to an end on what had dawned as another perfect day*

on their little farm on this idyllic island jaime conchita and the rest of the community of two hundred souls believed that they had been visited on by devine retribution about eleven oclock in the morning the sky had clouded over and then the sky became increasingly dark until it was darker than any night because there was no moon to give them even the faintest of light both jaime and his wife had fallen to their knees and cried out god forgive us and save our children but to no avail as the darkness lasted for two hours although it had seemed to them to have lasted for a lifetime when at last it was over for of course the sun had not disappeared it had been nothing more than a total eclipse of the sun everyone was so relieved the little community decided to invite a priest to come to their island paradise and to build a little church so that they could show god they still had faith and to ensure that they would be given heavenly protection in the future

(See the suggested solution.)

Methods of written communication

The term 'written communication' is a catch-all one for a whole range of methods of recording information. It obviously does not mean 'hand-written', purely and simply, although that is one of the methods.

Nowadays such a large amount of communication takes place by telephone that it almost seems as if the written forms of communication have taken a back seat and are in danger of becoming a minor part of the business world. That is very far from the truth and there are a number of very important reasons for this.

- As organizations grow larger and more complex they have a greater need for internal communication which is permanently recorded. This excludes electronic mail.
- The growth in importance of quality assurance systems has meant that more records are kept. This also accounts for the growing need to write standard operating procedures.
- The growth in the importance of training and formal qualifications has led to the increase in the number of in-house training programmes, which have to be written down for the benefit of all who are involved in them.

- Although letter writing has been replaced to a great extent by the fax (facsimile) machine, this in turn has meant that those letters which do have to be written, are done in a way which reflects the high quality of the organization.

The methods of written communication which will be covered in this book will be as follows:

- internal memos;
- telephone messages;
- reports;
- business letters;
- keeping records;
- summarizing.

The internal memorandum (the memo)

Much of the tedious nature of memos has been removed by microchip technology in the form of the word processor, but whether your memo is being sent via the electronic mail or on a memo format makes no difference. The style of language and the choice of vocabulary are just as important whichever method is chosen. An example of a typical memo format is reproduced in Figure 2, but organizations will always try to put their own individual stamp on their stationery, so styles will differ.

Whatever the style chosen by an organization, an internal memo should always contain certain information:

- the name of the person or persons to whom it is addressed;
- the name of the person who has originated it;
- the date;
- a subject heading;
- the text.

It is only fair to point out that a memorandum is not always a short message for internal distribution, but can be a lengthy document which is nothing less than a report. However, the majority of memos are simply short messages for internal use and are usually written in a style which verges on the blunt, even when someone is asking another to do something for them.

Memorandum

To:

From:

Date:

Ref:

HEADING (if there is one)

Paragraph xxxxxxxxxxxxxxxxxxxxxxxxxxxxxxxxxxxxxxxxxxxxxxxxxxxxxxxxxxxxxxxxxxxxxxxxxxxxxxx
xxxxxxxxxxxxxxxxxxxxxxxxxxxxxxxxxxxxxxxxxxxxxxxxxxxxxxxxxxxxxxxxxxxxxxxxxxxxxxxxxxxxxxxxxxx
xxxxxxxxxxxxxxxxxxxxxxx

Paragraph xxxxxxxxxxxxxxxxxxxxxxxxxxxxxxxxxxxxxxxxxxxxxxxxxxxxxxxxxxxxxxxxxxxxxxxxxxxxxxx
xxxxxxxxxxxxxxxxxxxxxxxxxxxxxxxxxxxxxxxxxxxxxxxxxxxxxxxxxxxxxxxxxxxxxxxxxxxxxxxxxxxxxxxxxxx
xxxxxxxxxxxxxxxxxxxxxxx

Fig. 2 A typical memo format

TASK 41 (L3)

You are a fairly junior assistant in the production planning department of a small but busy machine tool firm in Suffolk, called Pheasant Machine Tools Ltd. The firm's address is Unit 24, Longmeadow Lane, Ipswich, Suffolk IP2 5TY.

Your duties include drawing up a schedule of work for the week based on the urgency of jobs in hand, as well as those which have just come in but which have not yet been started.

In order to draw up the schedule, you have to obtain an indication of the availability of the machines and labour from each of the seven sections which comprise this small company, which you then transfer on to a kind of wall planner, or wall diary which can be used to match up the jobs for the week.

The chart shows at a glance how many hours are available for each machine and employee in each of the seven sections for each day of the week, from Monday to Friday. The chart is then given to your manager together with a brief report in writing supporting the information on the chart, first thing on Monday morning. That means that your information has to be collected from each of the seven sections on Friday afternoon.

A new assistant, Jim Johnson, has just joined the firm and it is your task to write a memo to him setting out clear instructions to him so that he will be able to carry out your current job of reporting machine and employee availability to the manager, Mr John Giles, every Monday.

The sections are: Tool room, five machines, supervisor Arthur Able; Lathe room, three machines, supervisor Fred Howland; Grinding room, three machines, foreman Bill Jarvis; Polishing room, two machines, foreman Ken Bell; Drawing office, five draughtsmen, manager Wilfred Smith; Engineering stores, three storemen, foreman Alex Irlam; Steel stock room, four storemen, foreman Peter Eaves.

The memorandum should show the processes you have to go through in order to produce both the chart and the report by Monday morning.

(There is no suggested solution for this task.)

Business letters

There are basically three styles of letter layout to choose from:

- indented;
- semi-blocked;
- fully blocked.

Examples of these are set out in Fig. 3.

No matter which format you choose, and that will normally be decided by the organization for which you work, there will be a number of conventions which have to be observed.

The reference

The words 'Our Ref:' and 'Your Ref:' are usually printed as part of the letterhead, and all that has to be added is the actual reference code which looks like TY/GH, the first two letters being the initials of the originator of the letter, and the other two, or more, will be the initials of the person who typed it. Sometimes it also has an additional code which could be that of a cost centre, department or project. It has been added to make the filing of the copy, and the retrieval of the correct file easier.

(a) Indented

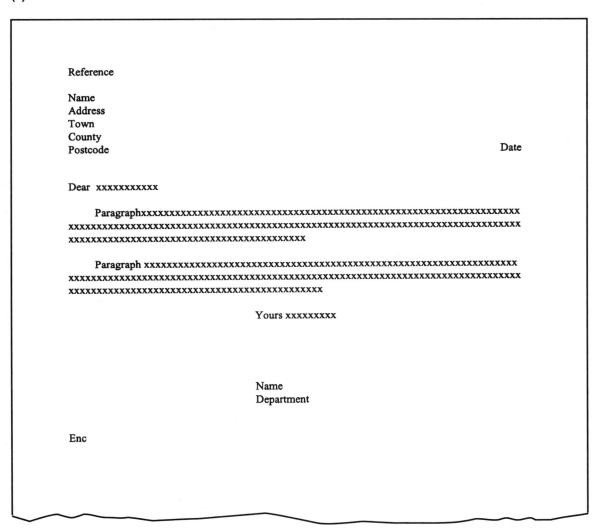

Reference

Name
Address
Town
County
Postcode   Date

Dear xxxxxxxxxxx

    Paragraphxxxxxxxxxxxxxxxxxxxxxxxxxxxxxxxxxxxxxxxxxxxxxxxxxxxxxxxxxxxxxxxxxx
xxxxxxxxxxxxxxxxxxxxxxxxxxxxxxxxxxxxxxxxxxxxxxxxxxxxxxxxxxxxxxxxxxxxxxxxxxxxxxx
xxxxxxxxxxxxxxxxxxxxxxxxxxxxxxxxxxxxxxxxxxxx

    Paragraph xxxxxxxxxxxxxxxxxxxxxxxxxxxxxxxxxxxxxxxxxxxxxxxxxxxxxxxxxxxxxxxxxxx
xxxxxxxxxxxxxxxxxxxxxxxxxxxxxxxxxxxxxxxxxxxxxxxxxxxxxxxxxxxxxxxxxxxxxxxxxxxxxxx
xxxxxxxxxxxxxxxxxxxxxxxxxxxxxxxxxxxxxxxxxxxxx

                         Yours xxxxxxxxx

                      Name
                      Department

Enc

Fig. 3 Styles of letter layout

The date

In Britain and the rest of Europe, usually, the date is written in the format:

day   month   year

It therefore appears as 14 August 1993. The only punctuation to appear in it is at the end of the year. Although we say 'The fourteenth' when we speak, we do not write 'th' after the figure 14.

(b) Semi-blocked

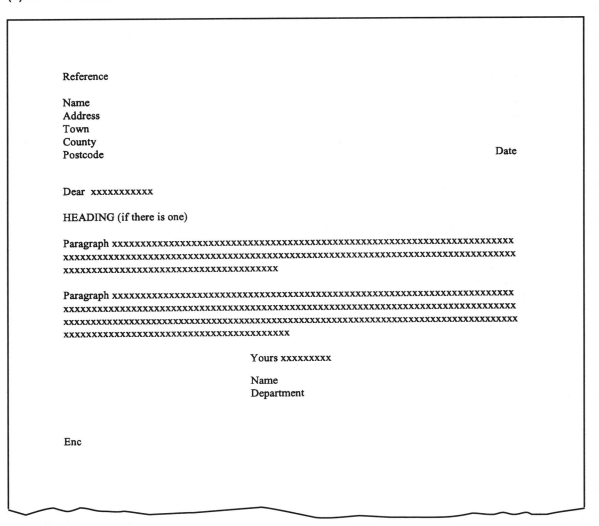

Reference

Name
Address
Town
County
Postcode   Date

Dear xxxxxxxxxxx

HEADING (if there is one)

Paragraph xxxxxxxxxxxxxxxxxxxxxxxxxxxxxxxxxxxxxxxxxxxxxxxxxxxxxxxxxxxxxxxxxxxxxxxxxxxx
xxxxxxxxxxxxxxxxxxxxxxxxxxxxxxxxxxxxxxxxxxxxxxxxxxxxxxxxxxxxxxxxxxxxxxxxxxxxxxxxxx
xxxxxxxxxxxxxxxxxxxxxxxxxxxxxxxxxxxxxxxxxx

Paragraph xxxxxxxxxxxxxxxxxxxxxxxxxxxxxxxxxxxxxxxxxxxxxxxxxxxxxxxxxxxxxxxxxxxxxxxxxxxx
xxxxxxxxxxxxxxxxxxxxxxxxxxxxxxxxxxxxxxxxxxxxxxxxxxxxxxxxxxxxxxxxxxxxxxxxxxxxxxxxxx
xxxxxxxxxxxxxxxxxxxxxxxxxxxxxxxxxxxxxxxxxxxxxxxxxxxxxxxxxxxxxxxxxxxxxxxxxxxxxxxxxx
xxxxxxxxxxxxxxxxxxxxxxxxxxxxxxxxxxxxxxxxxxx

                                         Yours xxxxxxxxx

                                         Name
                                         Department

Enc

Fig. 3 Styles of letter layout (continued)

In the USA the convention is somewhat different, in that they write the date with the month first: August 14 1993; but then, that is the way they would say the date in normal speech.

Titles and styles of address

The most commonly used styles of address are as follows:

For men:	*Mr, Esq. Rev, Sir, Lord*
For women:	*Mrs, Miss, Ms, Lady, Dame*

(c) Fully blocked

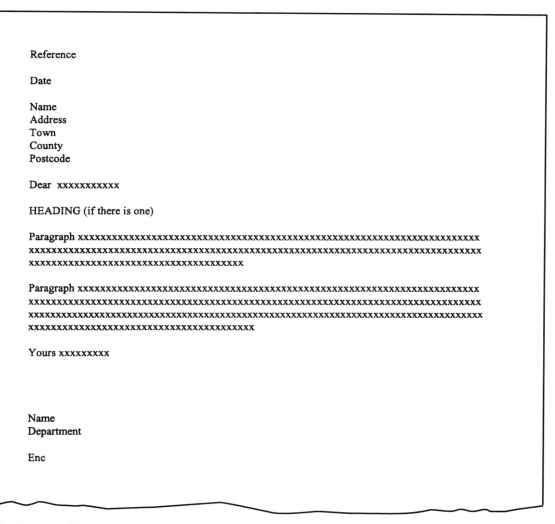

Reference

Date

Name
Address
Town
County
Postcode

Dear xxxxxxxxxxx

HEADING (if there is one)

Paragraph xxxxxxxxxxxxxxxxxxxxxxxxxxxxxxxxxxxxxxxxxxxxxxxxxxxxxxxxxxxxxxxxxxxxxxxxxx
xxxxxxxxxxxxxxxxxxxxxxxxxxxxxxxxxxxxxxxxxxxxxxxxxxxxxxxxxxxxxxxxxxxxxxxxxxxxxxxxxxxxxx
xxxxxxxxxxxxxxxxxxxxxxxxxxxxxxxxxxxxxxxxx

Paragraph xxxxxxxxxxxxxxxxxxxxxxxxxxxxxxxxxxxxxxxxxxxxxxxxxxxxxxxxxxxxxxxxxxxxxxxxxx
xxxxxxxxxxxxxxxxxxxxxxxxxxxxxxxxxxxxxxxxxxxxxxxxxxxxxxxxxxxxxxxxxxxxxxxxxxxxxxxxxxxxxx
xxxxxxxxxxxxxxxxxxxxxxxxxxxxxxxxxxxxxxxxxxxxxxxxxxxxxxxxxxxxxxxxxxxxxxxxxxxxxxxxxxxxxx
xxxxxxxxxxxxxxxxxxxxxxxxxxxxxxxxxxxxxxxxxxx

Yours xxxxxxxxx

Name
Department

Enc

Fig. 3 Styles of letter layout (continued)

One that is used for either men or women is Dr (Doctor) (and more recently, Rev (Reverend)).

When you are writing to registered companies, public corporations etc., there is no need to put anything before the name of the organization. The one exception to this is where you are writing to a partnership, such as a medical practice or a firm of accountants. The convention there is to use 'Messrs' which is short for 'messieurs', the French for 'gentlemen'. However, its use is declining, and it might even cause offence if the partnership you are writing to consists of a mixture of men and women.

The address of the recipient

Although there is nothing wrong in addressing a letter to an organization, the chances of it ending up on the desk of the right person are much less than if you make the effort to find out the name of the person who would normally deal with the subject you are writing about. As well as the name you should also include his or her job title or department:

Dr Julia Davidson
Head of Biological Sciences
University of Warwick
Archibald Campus
Warwick
CO14 4HJ

In the above example you have the correct title, name of the person and the department. Note also that the address has the postcode on the last line, by itself. This is because it makes it easier for the Post Office to sort the mail and should help to speed up delivery.

Initial salutations and complimentary closes

Salutation	Complimentary close
Dear Sir	Yours faithfully
Dear Madam	ditto
Dear Mr Andrews	Yours sincerely
Dear Mrs Smith	ditto
Dear Miss Welsh	ditto
Dear Dr Richards	ditto
Dear Rev Brooks	ditto
Dear Lord Brabazon	ditto
Dear Sir John	ditto
Dear Lady Allenby	ditto
Dear Fred	Kind regards
Dear Alice	ditto
My Dear Beth	Best wishes/Love
My Dear Bob	ditto

As you will see from the list, the more friendly two correspondents are the less formal the close becomes, and in fact it can take almost any form which is mutually acceptable.

The structure of letters

Following on from the salutation there is usually a subject or content heading, which is underlined, or put in bold type. This acts as an announcement in much the same way as a newspaper headline does, and it tells the reader in brief form what the letter is about.

The text of the letter is broken up into paragraphs, each of which has a particular function. The *first paragraph* sets out the context of the letter by referring to previous dates, times, personnel or correspondence relating to the subject or purpose of the letter. The *middle paragraph(s)* deal with the subject of the letter in detail, each paragraph containing a separate subject or development of the same subject. The purpose in doing so is to make it easier on the reader to recognize the progression, and to help him or her to separate individual points. Consider the example on page 92.

Woodford Electronics plc
Nash House
Regents Park Road
London
NW1 3GC

Telephone: 081-656 3434
Facsimile: 081-221 4675

Our Ref: TRY/GH Mktg45
Your Ref: AL/RE

24 July 199-

Dr A Lambton
Comgraph Superstores Ltd
546 Marylebone High Street
London
WC2 6YT

Dear Dr Lambton

The New Range of Magichord Keyboards

It was delightful to meet you again at the recent Electronics Fair in Birmingham, and to be able to show you our new range of keyboards in which you expressed an interest.

As I promised you at the fair, I am sending you a full set of sales literature which I am sure you will find both eye-catching and informative. As I explained to you at the time, the range has been taken up by some of the biggest chains of retail distributors in the country, to say nothing of the response from European customers.

The technology and design are outstanding, and I am sure that they cannot be matched even by the Japanese, who are our closest rivals. As far as price is concerned, we know we are very competitive even without any initial discount which might be offered for stocking a new range.

Knowing how keen you were to start a new line, and given the very wide distribution network which you offer any manufacturer, I should like to offer you a starter order, which will be much smaller than you might otherwise consider, but which will minimize the risk of stocking a new line. As part of the starter order you will be given preferential discount rates, and immediate delivery to any number of branch destinations you would like.

I feel sure that you will want to take advantage of this offer in time to coincide with our national TV advertising campaign, and look forward to hearing from you in due course.
Yours sincerely

Tom Young
Marketing Director

The style and language of letters

The English language has the advantage of being very rich in vocabulary. No matter what you want to say, there are usually a number of different ways that it can be said, each with its own subtle shade of meaning. The reason for this phenomenon is the variety of different languages which make up the English language, and it is perfectly possible to be as persuasive as it is to be precise. Look at the following two approaches to the use of language:

Objective and factual	Subjective and emotive
To explain / inform	*To be persuasive*
To report	*To motivate*
To confirm	*To get co-operation*
To list facts	*To sell*

From the style of the letter in the example above, it is obvious that its purpose is to sell the company's products. Not only do we get that message from the words used, but also from the open, friendly and persuasive tone of the letter. Now look at the letter that follows and decide what it is trying to achieve.

Rowlands Antiques
CURIO CORNER
THE BAILEYHEAD
OSWESTRY
SHROPSHIRE
SY11 3VB

Tel: OSWESTRY 336574

15 March 199–

Lt Colonel Smythe-Waters
The Copse
Dummer Clump
Hants
RG45 2DF

Dear Colonel Smythe-Waters

Outstanding Account for Jacobean Blanket Chest - £385

Once again I have to trouble you to settle your account for the Jacobean Blanket Chest which you purchased from me in November of last year.

I know that you have been on a tour of duty abroad, but now that you are back, I feel that it would be an ideal opportunity to settle this account which has been outstanding for a little too long now.

I have managed to obtain two matching Jacobean chairs for you but on the advice of my solicitor, and my bank manager, I feel that I cannot let you have them until your outstanding account is clear.

In fact, my solicitor has also advised me that I should tell you that unless it is paid by 15 April, I should then leave it in his hands to deal with.

I feel sure that it will not be necessary to do that and I look forward to receiving your cheque in the very near future.

Yours sincerely

Clive Baines
Proprietor

If you thought that Clive was after money, and that should not have been so difficult to spot, then you were right. But he was not as matter-of-fact as some organizations might be when it comes to asking for money. The reason is that if the Colonel pays up Clive will more than likely make another sale, so his style of breaking the bad news about being determined to collect the overdue account is rather gentle and persuasive.

Points to remember

- *Be firm but polite:*

  I feel that I cannot let you have (the chairs) until your account has been cleared.

  Don't say:

  I know the account is not very much, but it is overdue by quite a lot and I'd be terribly grateful if you could see your way to sending us something towards it.

- *Be persuasive:*

  I am sure that you will find our products to be of the highest quality without being uncompetitive.

  Don't say:

  I think what we've got is reasonably good for the price, although not everyone thinks so.

- *Be helpful:*

  No matter what the problem is likely to be, we shall always be available to attend to it for you.

  Don't say:

  I read your letter about the motor in the appliance you bought here but I really don't know when we'll be able to get round to have a look at it, but we'll try our best.

- *Keep things simple:*

  I'm sorry the holiday you booked with us has no hotel rooms available. We shall refund your money immediately, unless you would like to consider an alternative.

Don't say:

> *The holiday destination which was chosen by you seems to be having some problems of a lack of availability due to there being more customers than rooms. Although refunds are a distinct possibility, we should be grateful if you would transfer your defunct reservation to another destination.*

Other traits which should be avoided at all costs are being too familiar with someone you do not know, allowing irrelevant information or comment to enter into the letter and the use of clichés.

TASK 42 (L2/3)

Your assistant has written the following letter to a customer and has asked you to check it before it is posted. There are a number of errors in it which you should note down.

Mr J. Williams esq.
43, Roman Walk,
Palacefields
Runcorn WA4 2LU
                                                                24 January 199-

Our ref: LP Coach-67
Weekend trip to Brussels - April 199-

Dear Sir

Thanks a lot for youre inquiry about a 45 seat coach to go to Brussels next April for a week end.

We don't usually do such short trips but given the poor economical climate at the present, we'll look favorably on your request.

The trip can be done on a weekend in April leaving Runcorn Old Town Center at 6 pm on Friday evening and arriving in Brussles, Hotel Minou, Grande Place at 1 pm on Saturday. The sea-crossing will be from Harwich to the Hook of Holland.

The coach will depart from the Hotel Minou on Monday evening at 7 pm for the return journey arriving in Runcorn at 12 noon on Tuesday.
The price per person will be £95 and will include the price of travel, two nights bed and break fast in the Hotel Minou and trip round Brussels to see the sites.

We hope this'll be exceptable to you and look forward to hearing from you soon.

Yours Sincerely,

(See the suggested solution.)

TASK 43 (L2/3)

Imagine you are the headteacher of a large comprehensive school and one of your pupils is a consistent truant. You have decided to have him transferred to a special unit which has been set up specifically to deal with such problems. You should write to the parents to tell them of your decision. Their name and address is:

>Mr and Mrs D Donaldson
>236 Lapwing Lane
>Balham
>London
>SW7 4FG.

(There is no suggested solution to this task.)

Writing simple reports

Although this section is about simple reports, it contains a number of features which also apply to much longer reports. The main difference between simple reports and longer ones is the length, and the fact that simple ones need less organizing than the others.

According to the *Concise Oxford Dictionary*, a report is an 'Account given or opinion formally expressed after investigation or consideration or collation of information; . . .' Quite rightly, the definition does not say that reports have to be written, but this chapter will concentrate on the written aspect. Before going on to how they should be tackled, consider for a few moments, what reasons there could be for writing them.

- *Routine reports*. These might be to do with planned maintenance programmes, safety inspections, sales reports, project progress reports or output performance reports.
- *Irregular or occasional reports*. Accident reports, discipline reports and damage reports.
- *Special purpose reports*. Changes in work methods, staff redundancy programme, feasibility studies and market research.

Report writing can be divided into four stages.

Stage 1. The reason for writing the report should be made clear to the reader at the earliest opportunity, and this is done by setting out terms of reference at the beginning.

Stage 2. The next stage of the report is a fact-gathering exercise to establish the present, or current situation. Included in that section of it should be a clear statement of the method employed in carrying out the investigation.

Stage 3. When all the fact gathering has been completed, the facts should be analyzed and conclusions drawn.

Stage 4. From the conclusions which have been drawn, recommendations should then be made.

What to include in a report

When it comes to writing up the report, certain information should always be supplied for the benefit of the reader(s).

1 The name or title
2 The author's name
3 The person who asked for the report
4 The date the report was written/presented
5 The contents, with page numbers
6 The terms of reference
7 An introduction
8 The methodology
9 The findings/conclusions
10 The recommendations
11 Appendices
12 Acknowledgements
13 A bibliography

Although it looks like a lot, not every item on the above list would appear on every report, and even those that do might be quite short, e.g. the appendices might only include two items. Some internal or inter-departmental reports are little more than extended memoranda, and might not contain more than a brief report on the status of some aspect of the business.

The style of language to adopt

- It should be written in a formal style, in the passive voice. In other words do not personalize it by using 'I' and 'we' statements.

- Keep to simple language, avoiding the use of jargon as far as possible. If you have to resort to jargon, make sure that someone who might be unfamiliar with it is given an explanation, perhaps in the form of a glossary.

- Avoid the use of contractions such as 'isn't', 'won't', 'didn't', etc.

- Make sure that each section is broken up into discrete paragraphs for ease of reading and understanding.

- If you use a word processor to produce the report, its layout and presentation can be very professional in appearance.

- Remember that a report is the presentation of facts. Do not make the mistake of drawing absurd conclusions from them, or of indulging in fantastic speculation. In a way, conclusions are opinions, but they are opinions which can be backed up by showing the clear link between cause and effect.

TASK 44 (L2/3)

Write a short report on the level of satisfaction/dissatisfaction that people have with the provision of refreshment facilities in your school, college or place of work. Collect your evidence by means of a questionnaire and ask as many people to answer your questions as possible. Assure them of its confidentiality. Present your report to someone in authority.

There is no suggested solution to this task but check with your tutor before presenting your report to anyone.

Summarizing

In order to make a successful summary of any document, you need to follow a plan. Such a plan should include:

- checking the aims;
- understanding the original text;

- identifying the main points;
- making an initial draft;
- writing a final version.

1   Make sure you understand what it is you are supposed to do. Some summaries are not to include every area covered in the original.

2   Make sure that you understand the original before you make any attempt to do a summary. This can only be achieved by reading the original two or three times so that at the end of it:
   — you will have absorbed its general meaning;
   — you will have checked the meaning of any words you do not know;
   — you will recognize the main points and understand why they have been developed in the way that they have.

3   Give the summary a title in the same way that you might give a letter a subject heading.

4   Pick out the main points of the document, making notes of each one in your own words. Compare all the points with the title you have chosen, to see if the match is good. Get rid of unnecessary detail at this stage, such as illustrations and examples which support the main points.

5   Check your list of points again when you have finished writing your notes. If anything has been forgotten, it should be included at this stage. Conversely, if there is something which is not needed, it should be cut out. When you write up your notes they will no doubt expand a little.

6   Prepare your rough draft. Before you start to write it, think about the best way to produce the summary, that is continuous prose form or a list of numbered sentences. If you are not sure which would be best, try both and see which one reads better. When you think you have finished the draft, go over the spelling, punctuation and grammar for mistakes.

7   Write the final version by copying it out carefully, taking great care not to miss out any important words, phrases or even paragraphs. This should not be a problem if you have access to a word processor as the information can be kept on disk and amended as and when necessary.

Summarizing is a brutal process, because you are going through the work that someone else has painstakingly created, and cutting great pieces out of it in order to make it the size you want. The smaller the final piece is to be relative to the original, the more brutal you will have to be.

TASK 45 (L2/3)

Read the following passage and try to pick out the main points from it. Reduce it to around sixty words.

> *On the coast road the trip eastwards to Rize is not nearly as grand as the one from Samsun to Giresun, but at least there is a large camp site by the sea, in the small town of Yomra, if you are interested in that sort of thing. All the little towns and villages along this stretch of coast are very similar.*
>
> *If you are expecting ancient Turkish houses exuding an air of antiquity, you are going to be sadly disappointed. Very few old Turkish houses are still standing, the majority of the buildings given over to dwelling houses are partly finished blocks of flats, standing sentinel over unmade streets. Such a dismal sounding place has the saving grace of having beautiful beaches, lapped by unpolluted water, which go all the way to the little village of Iyidere. (135 words)*

(See the suggested solution.)

3

Communicating without words

This chapter covers Elements 2.3 and 3.3.

The overall aim of Elements 2.3 and 3.3 is to ensure that students can use images to illustrate points made in writing and in discussions with a range of people on a variety of subjects.

OBJECTIVES

At the end of the elements, students will be able to use images:

1 which will support both the main and the minor points in the communication which the audience may have difficulty in understanding;

2 which will provide a clear illustration of the point(s) to which they refer;

3 at points which are appropriate.

The kinds of images used may be sketches, diagrams, photographs or charts.

Using illustrations

Communicating without words seems to suggest that we are about to become involved in body language, but this is not the case. The kind of non-verbal communication referred to by the title of this chapter involves tables, charts and even photographs. It does not mean to say that words are completely abandoned, although communication *is* sometimes enhanced by the lack of them. The examples below show what is meant by that claim.

Fig. 4 Words are not always necessary

The signs are effective because everyone knows what they mean, but also because they are quite easy to work out anyway.

Drawings

There is a difference when it comes to making use of drawings and sketches, because they have to be accompanied by words for them to be effective.

TASK 46 (L2)

By way of illustrating this point, look at the drawing which appears on page 106 and try to put a caption to it. There is no right answer to this simple task, because we all perceive such things differently. However, as soon as a caption is attached to it, we concentrate on the extent to which the message in the words is augmented by the drawing.

What caption would you put to his drawing?

Nowadays drawings are not usually used in as straightforward a way as they used to be thirty or forty years ago. At that time it was quite common for a newspaper advertisement to include a simple drawing as a way of bringing the advertiser's message to life. By contrast, today's advertisers make use of drawings in a much more imaginative way, often in a more fantastic way too.

Photographs

Photographs are quite a different matter. Some forty years ago the number of photographs to appear in a newspaper, or any other publication was quite small, but now we are surrounded by them at every turn. Holiday brochures rely heavily on the power of the colour photograph to sell their holiday destinations.

Another use to which photographs can be put is in hairdressing salons, to show clients how good they can look when they have a particular style or other treatment.

Fig. 5 Colour photographs are used to sell holidays

We are so used to the visual image in present-day life, especially through television, that we think nothing of seeing photographs used in their hundreds to sell all kinds of products in, for example, a mail-order catalogue.

Fig. 6 Photographs are used to sell a huge variety of products

Charts and tables

Flowcharts

One of the most effective uses for charts is the 'flowchart', which can be adapted to a wide range of activities. As a way of describing the logical way to tackle a job, whether easy or difficult, the flowchart is extremely useful. An example of a flowchart for the simple task of turning on a television set is shown below. The symbols used in the construction of flowcharts are very simple but effective.

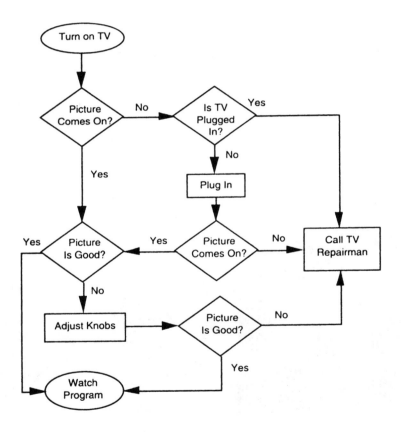

Fig. 7 A flowchart for turning on a television set

You will see that the ovals represent activities, the boxes represent processes and the diamonds represent decisions which have to be made. The flowchart presents two scenarios, the first is where a process follows the path it ought to, and the second is where the process follows some undesired path. The next flowchart shows the process of administration in the emergency department of a hospital.

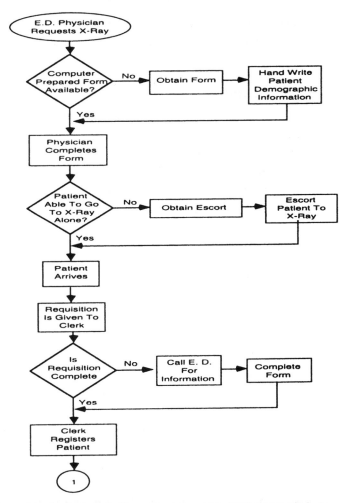

Fig. 8 A flowchart showing the process of administration in a hospital emergency department

Here are some tips for constructing and interpreting a flowchart.

- Define the boundaries of the process clearly.
- Use only the simplest symbols.
- Make sure that every feedback loop has an escape.
- Usually a process box has only one output arrow; otherwise it may require a decision diamond.

TASK 47 (L2/3)

Practise drawing flowcharts by choosing a simple everyday activity and converting it into one. But do not choose 'switching on the television'!

There is no suggested solution to this task for obvious reasons. When you have completed the task, check your solution with your tutor.

Pareto charts

A pareto chart is a special form of vertical bar graph which helps to determine which problems to solve and in what order they should be dealt with. The data collected from whatever source are displayed in such a way that we can tell at a glance that we shall gain the most by tackling the problems represented by the tallest bar. An example is shown in Figure 9.

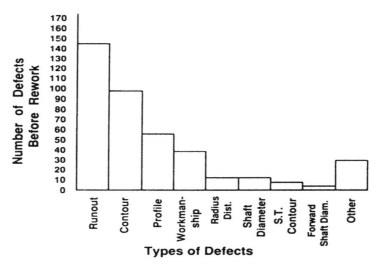

Fig. 9 A pareto chart (for defects found at an in-process inspection)

To construct a pareto chart, take the following steps:

1 Select the problems that are to be compared and put into rank order.

2 Select the standard unit of measurement to be compared, e.g. annual cost, frequency, etc.

3 Select the time period to be studied, e.g. 8 hours, 7 days, 4 weeks.

4 Gather the necessary data for each of the categories chosen, e.g. 'Defect A occurred X times during the last week'.

5   Compare the frequency or cost of each category relative to all other categories.

6   List the categories from left to right on the horizontal axis in their order of decreasing frequency or cost. The categories containing the fewest items can be combined into an 'other' category which is placed on the extreme right of the last bar.

7   Above each category or classification, draw a rectangle whose height represents the frequency or cost in that classification.

Frequency of fault or problem can be converted into cost and a chart for each one constructed. This will show that the most frequently encountered fault or problem is not always the most costly. Such a discovery can result in making a decision about whether to tackle a problem on the basis of frequency or cost.

The histogram

The histogram is a bar chart similar to a pareto chart except that it displays different information in a different way. The pareto chart deals with characteristics of a product or service, e.g. the type of fault or problem, while a histogram displays a measurement and displays its distribution. All repeated events will produce results that vary over time, and a histogram reveals the amount of variation that any process has within it.

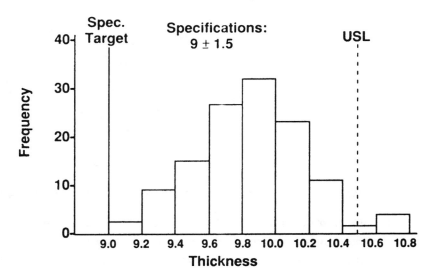

Fig. 10 A histogram

Figure 10 is a histogram showing the thickness data of a class of product, the frequency of which is measured by means of a stroke record. It shows the central tendency, in this case a thickness of between 9.80 and 9.99. Also, if a line is drawn through the centre of the tops of the rectangles, it produces a curve which displays properties close to what is called a normal distribution of frequency, in other words, a bell-shaped curve.

The pie chart

Yet another way of displaying statistical information is to do so by means of a pie chart. Pie charts are simply charts which are converted into circles which represent 100% (not 360 degrees)of the data to be displayed. The circle, or pie, is then divided into percentage slices that show clearly the largest shares of data. The pie chart is at least as useful as a pareto chart, if not more so, as can be seen by the number of times it is used to show comparisons of data in the newspapers, or on television. As with all other graphs, be sure to label the subject matter clearly with dates (if necessary), the percentages within the slices, and what each slice represents.

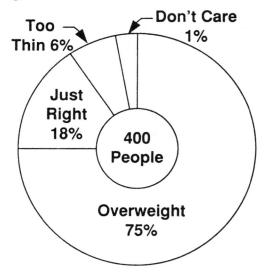

Fig. 11 A pie chart (from a survey of feelings on weight)

Remember that all of these methods of displaying data are nothing more than aids to illustrate the main presentation. They simply compare or highlight data in a particular format; they do not interpret it.

TASK 48 (L2/3)

In your school, college or place of work ask for volunteers to have their height measured and compared with their age and sex. Construct a chart of this information, and convert it into:

1 a histogram;

2 a pie chart.

Write a short report on any conclusions which you can draw from the data collected. Make sure that your histogram and your pie chart are supported by a graph of your data. There is no suggested solution to this task, but you should have something which resembles the examples provided. Ask your tutor to check the accuracy of your solution.

4

Making a response

This chapter covers Elements 2.4 and 3.4.

The overall aim of Elements 2.4 and 3.4 is to ensure that students can read and respond to written material and images on a range of routine and other matters.

OBJECTIVES

At the end of the elements, students will be able to respond to written material and images on routine and other matters and:

1 identify accurately the main points;

2 identify accurately the meanings of unfamiliar words, phrases and images using appropriate sources of clarification.

Communication from other people comes in a great many ways, each one of which is chosen to produce a particular effect, such as:

- to inform;
- to highlight;
- to compare;
- to reveal;
- to amuse;
- to persuade; or
- to entice.

Unfortunately, the information which we receive from others is not neatly labelled with its purpose so we have to arm ourselves with knowledge about the techniques being employed by the originator so that we are fully aware of his or her intention.

Look at the example on page 118.

Memorandum

To: All hourly paid employees
From: Simon Albright, Managing Director.

Date: 24 July 19-

Subject: Redundancy Programme

In view of the lengthy discussions which have taken place with the unions over the past few months, and the continued failure of the economy to provide an upturn in our business, it has been decided to set up a programme for redundancy of some hourly paid employees.

It has been agreed with the unions that, as far as possible, no compulsory redundancies will be made. All redundancies will be on a voluntary basis and the company will be looking for volunteers to come forward from certain preferred sections of the work force.

The preferred areas have been identified as follows:

- hourly paid employees over the age of fifty;
- hourly paid employees who are in the two lowest pay grades;
- those employees in any grade who have a chronic health problem.

The rate of redundancy payment will be a multiple of the statutory rate and will be announced within the next two weeks. There will also be a lump sum payment given to all employees who accept a redundancy offer.

Anyone who is interested in applying for voluntary redundancy should indicate their interest by filling in the appropriate form available from the Personnel Department. All applications will be treated in the strictest confidence.

S Albright

S Albright, Managing Director

The principal purpose of the memo is to give information to employees. It also gives information which may or may not be intentional, but which is nevertheless interesting.

- It mentions the category of employees who are going to be favoured in the selection of volunteers.
- It is no mistake that the lowest paid employees are among that group because the rate of redundancy will be calculated on their average earnings, probably over a period of the last year.
- By singling out employees with chronic health problems it is obvious that the cost of employing such people is looked on as unacceptable.

In this example the information in it which was intended to be passed on, was stated in a matter-of-fact way. Sometimes the originator of a piece of information wants part of it to be noticed more than any other, and this is achieved in a variety of ways.

TASK 49 (L2/3)

Look at the examples which are produced in Fig. 12 on page 120 and make a list of the information which you think the originator of the communication feels is more important than the rest of it. When you think you have done that successfully, make up your own example of communication which highlights certain information.

After having looked at the examples provided so far, and having made up your own example, you should now be quite skilled at identifying the message in a variety of forms of communication. Look at the examples and make a really comprehensive list of the features in each example which identify certain pieces of information in a particular way.

- Which one tries to persuade you to do something and how does it do it?
- Which one tries to amuse you, and so on?

With some kinds of communication, particularly textbooks, the vocabulary which is used can be quite specialized and almost unintelligible to

Anthony's Travel

LUXURY MINI COACHES FOR ALL OCCASIONS

28 VICTORIA ROAD . RUNCORN . CHESHIRE . WA7 5BH
TELEPHONE . 0928 561460

Dear Sir/Madam,

We would like to take this opportunity of introducing ourselves to you.

Anthony's Travel are currently operating luxury Mini-Coaches of a capacity of twelve, fourteen, sixteen and nineteen seat vehicles with television, video, drinks machine and P.A. system.

In addition a 52 seat Coach, or a 40 seat Coach with six tables for extra comfort, with video, toilet, reclining seats, refreshments/drinks machine and hostess if required.

We endeavour to provide a reliable, efficient service at competitive prices.

Our vehicles are available for all types of contract and private hire, day trips, nights out and airport connections. Our Executive Coaches are ideal to transport business clients, to create the right impression for your business. The comfort of these larger Coaches makes them ideal for touring holidays.

Should you require a quotation or any additional information please do not hesitate to contact us.

Yours faithfully

R.A. Bamber
ANTHONY'S TRAVEL

SIMPLY THE BEST !
Travel in Style

V.A.T. REG. NO. 483 4574 19

(a)

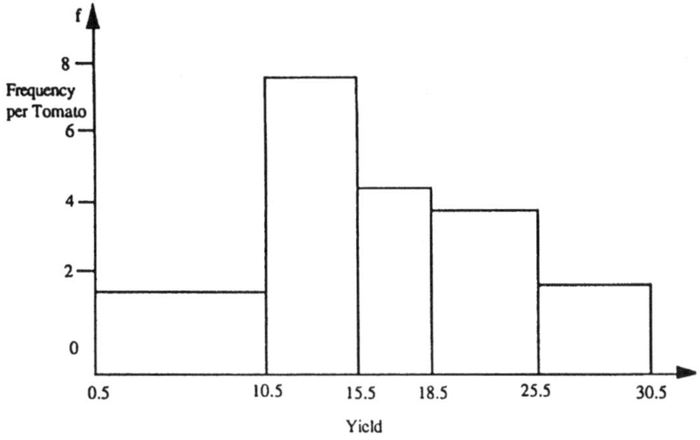
f
Frequency per Tomato
0
2
4
6
8
0.5
10.5
15.5
18.5
25.5
30.5
Yield

(b)

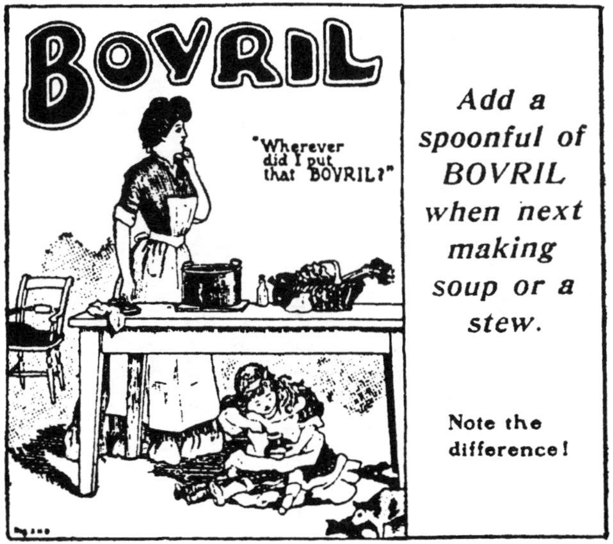
BOVRIL
"Wherever did I put that BOVRIL?"
Add a spoonful of BOVRIL when next making soup or a stew.
Note the difference!

(c)

Fig. 12

the reader who is not familiar with the jargon. In some cases it almost looks as if the originator of the piece has set out to conceal the information which exists behind the unfamiliar terminology.

TASK 50 (L3)

Read the following extract from a textbook and answer the questions related to it.

He saw his mission of running the RAC as an efficient and profitable business clouded by tradition and beset by embedded practices. His objective was to transform the RAC into a business-minded organization.

The problem facing the organization was, however, that in 1988, the volume of calls from motorists exceeded the capacity of the RAC's paper-based system. The RAC had little management information coming back from the system and no effective way of controlling the business or of monitoring its performance.

The RAC divided the country up into 17 autonomous regions, each with its own control room. Members had a card with 34 different emergency phone numbers. Only if they called the right number would they get through to the control area that could help.

A number of advisory committees dedicated to changing the whole direction of the company were formed. Recruiting new members, making a profit and becoming a high-tech company were set as the new goals. Corporate objectives and targets were issued to everyone and updated annually. Staff were encouraged to adopt a more informal and friendly style, more attuned to a modern company.

During Large's (Chief Executive) tenure at the RAC unnecessary levels of management were axed. The Marketing and Sales Departments spawned selling teams to sell bulk membership to car manufacturers, securing deals that would be the basis for phenomenal growth. The Personnel Department was charged with sorting out internal communications, and a computerized rescue service, based on a fully automated and nationally integrated network, was brought into place, known as the CARS system (Computer Assisted Rescue System).

In the context of the above passage, what is meant by the following words and phrases?

1 mission

2 efficient and profitable

3 clouded by tradition

4 beset

5 embedded practices

6 paper-based system

7 autonomous regions

8 dedicated to changing . . .

9 corporate objectives

10 attuned to . . .

11 charged with sorting out . . .

12 nationally integrated network

(See the suggested solution.)

The problem with word meanings is that a large number become associated with a particular incident, event or action. The fact that it has a discrete meaning is often forgotten. Where there is some doubt about the meaning of a word the most effective way of resolving it is to look the word up in the dictionary.

When the reverse is the case, that you have an idea or concept to express but cannot think of an appropriate word, there is a very useful book called *Roget's Thesaurus* which allows you to look for alternative words which may be more appropriate than the one you have thought of, and words which express ideas.

Assignment

As part of the assessment of your work on a GNVQ course, you have to do a piece of work which will demonstrate that you are competent in the areas which are covered by the Core Skills.

In your school, college or place of work, identify a problem area to which you feel you could find a solution. Hold a meeting with four or five members of your peer group to discuss the problem and its solution. Suggestions for topics include:

- Poor or inadequate canteen facilities
- Substandard classroom/workroom facilities
- Poor level of resources for teaching/working
- Understocked/understaffed library
- Inadequate car parking facilities
- A lack of creche facilities in college/work
- A lack of recreation facilities

Before proceeding with the project, an action plan should be written down in accordance with GNVQ requirements.

The meeting should be conducted in a formal way and minutes should be taken as a record of what was said.

At the end of the meeting a proposed solution and a method of accomplishing it should be proposed.

Each member of the meeting should be allotted a specific task to carry out.

After the exercise has been carried out:

1 The group should have contacted someone in authority by telephone and/or letter in order to arrange to present them with the problem and its solution.

2 The group should have given a presentation to a person or persons in authority stating the problem and its solution.

3 The group should have made use of the following presentation skills:

- a common written report of the problem and its solution;
- a verbal presentation using one example of each of the following: flip charts, OHPs, handouts, charts, graphs, photos, tape/slide presentations or video.

4 Each group member's report should include:

- a copy of every letter sent by any group member together with the reply;
- a reference to every book, journal, other document or radio or TV broadcast used, together with a short resumé of its relevance to the report.

5 The report should show evidence of the gathering and analysis of statistical information.

6 The report should be written using information technology.

Suggested solutions

Chapter 1

TASK 1

- The man might have taken offence at the tone of voice you used to speak to him.
- He might have taken offence at being addressed as 'mate'.
- He might be a stranger in the building himself.
- He might have been too busy to give you directions.
- He might hold an important position in the organization and not be used to people approaching him in such a direct way.
- He might also be a new employee who does not know the answer to your question.

TASK 2

'I'm sorry to trouble you but I'm lost and I wonder if you could tell me how to get to the Accounts Department?' You may have chosen other words but they should be polite and respectful without being subservient.

TASK 3

There are a number of ways of doing this, depending on the culture of your place of work.

You could ask for an appointment to see Mr Wilson, but that could be perceived as going above the head of your store manager, which is what you would be doing, in fact.

Make no mistake that what you plan to do involves a certain amount of risk, so it is best to wait until the right moment presents itself.

- Mr. Wilson should not be with a lot of people.
- He should not be deep in discussion with other important people.

You should go right up to him and face him; do not approach him from an angle or from behind, and you should say something like:

Mr Wilson, I have an idea for improving customer service and giving us an edge over our competitors, which I'd like to tell you about. There is an area of the store which could easily be converted to accommodate a children's play area.

At this point it is as well to pause for some sort of reaction to see if it is worth while your going on. It is not possible to anticipate accurately how the interview might continue because there are too many unpredictable variables, but you have achieved the following.

- You have made him aware that you exist and have thought about the good of the store.
- By facing him directly, you prevented him from escaping.
- You stated your case as briefly as possible, without leaving out any vital information.

TASK 4

'Mrs Thompson, I'm given 45 minutes to do the petty cash on a Friday, but it takes longer than that just to enter all of the petty cash vouchers and the receipts that haven't got vouchers. Then I have to balance the account, which is difficult because somebody has always taken the wrong amount due, and I have to find that error.'

You could go on to suggest an alternative way of dealing with the petty cash, or, you could wait for Mrs Thompson's reaction before saying any more. What you have done is to give the reason for the delay without making it sound like an excuse. You have also mentioned weaknesses in the system:

- more than one person seems to have access to the petty cash;
- people do not seem to operate the system properly;
- instead of entering the vouchers in the book as the cash is given out, it is left until the end of the week, making it more difficult for mistakes to be detected.

TASK 5

Since this task is more about tone of voice and manner than about the actual words you might use, you should have taken into account the fact that you need to talk to the children in a firm but pleasant tone. The task should be done in the form of a game with the suggestion that speed and efficiency are the most important goals to aim for.

TASK 6

She might react in any one of a number of ways:

- She might react angrily, and call you inconsiderate.
- She might ask you to see her later in the office.
- She might simply refuse to allow you to do it.

As you may have noticed, all of the reactions are negative ones. Another element has been introduced here, and that is the relationship between the employer and the employee – a question of status and different priorities.

TASK 7

There are far too many distractions for Mrs Glover to be able to take in what is being said to her. Each child has to be considered individually and all the parents who arrive have to be considered as well.

You should wait for a quiet moment when you will have Mrs Glover's full attention. Also, make sure that what you say is in the form of a *request*, rather than a statement or a demand. This indicates respect for Mrs Glover and is more likely to result in a favourable response.

TASK 8

If Gill likes to express her feelings immediately, she is likely to show how angry she is at being patronized. If she is more reticent, she may become sulky or sarcastic.

Alex could have said:

Gill, I know it's asking a lot, but I need this report before the meeting this afternoon, could you do it for me please?

Although he is an assistant manager, it's always better to ask people to do things rather than to give them orders. Other factors to consider are:

- Gill does not work exclusively for Alex.
- The status of assistant managers is often not much more than that of senior clerical workers.
- By typing the report for Alex, Gill will feel that the decision was hers and that it was not imposed on her.

TASK 9

1 Mrs Higgins' impression of Anderson-Wells is likely to be that it is a rather casual company, not very caring.
2 The company's reputation will have been damaged as a result of the treatment Mrs Higgins received at reception, no matter how good the company's products are.

3 • Angela should have familiarized herself with all the relevant details about Mrs Higgins before contacting anyone.

• Her manner should have been more polite and formal when she first spoke to Mrs Higgins, thus avoiding giving offence.

• She should not have called Mrs Higgins 'love'.

• She should not have called the Sales Director 'Wilf' in front of Mrs Higgins, even if it was normal to do so at other times.

• She should not have called Mrs Higgins 'she' on the telephone when Mrs Higgins was within earshot. By saying 'Says she's got an appointment . . .', it sounds as if Angela is implying Mrs Higgins might not be telling the truth.

• Angela should have got the Sales Director to meet Mrs Higgins at reception.

4 Angela is of lower status than Mrs Higgins.

5 Any employee of Anderson-Wells should treat Mrs Higgins as being of higher status than the company because she is a buyer from a potential customer.

TASK 10

There could be a number of contributory factors, such as:

• They feel that others will expect it.

• They want to behave differently in the new situation.

• They may want to emulate someone they admire in a similar situation to their new one.

• It could have been hinted to them that their new situation would call for a change in behaviour.

TASK 11

Tony Bold should have borne in mind that he wanted to get three vital pieces of information over to his work force:

1 Company profitability has dropped.

2 The productivity of every employee will have to improve.

3 The budgets in some areas will have to be reduced.

Tony's talk should have been more along the following lines:

In order to ensure the continued support of the shareholders of the company, the interest they get from their investment has to be maintained. If not, they might take their capital out of the business.

With the full co-operation of you all, I intend to carry out new staff appraisals which will result in everyone having to agree to higher targets as an important step towards improving profitability.

Another area where profitability can be improved is through stricter budgetary controls. Budgets are too generous in some areas, but all budgets are going to have to be reviewed, so I'll be talking to individual sections about their budgets over the next two weeks.

If anyone has any fears about being made redundant, I would like to reassure you all that there are no plans to do so and the threat need never arise provided we all agree to put in a little extra effort. I thank you all for your attention.

TASK 12

There is no suggested solution to Task 12

TASK 13

1 Grammar

On the first line, the word 'see' used in that form is an indicator of the importance of the statement immediately preceding it, but it is not grammatically correct because it is not connected to either a subject or an object.

'we wasn't' should be 'we weren't'. 'Was' is the simple past tense of the verb 'to be' for the first and third person singular, whereas 'we' is the first person plural.

2 Bad pronunciation

'Anythink' should be 'anything', and 'ast' should be 'asked'.

3 Improper use of words

'nor' is part of the two word negative comparative 'neither . . . nor', but in the sentence has been used instead of the word 'than' which is a conjunction used in expressions of comparative quantity, size, etc.

'pay raise' should be 'pay rise'. 'To raise' means to set something upright, to build up, to put on a higher position, to levy and to call up. However, it is acceptable in the USA and Canada. The accepted British English version is 'rise', which has the same connotation as 'increase'.

a If the sentence had been spoken in front of a peer group who spoke in the same way, then they would probably treat it as normal speech.

b A member of the senior management team might accept the way of speaking as normal for the person who uttered it because he or she might have pigeon-holed the speaker as belonging to a particular social class. But if the speaker was supposed to be of equal status to the senior manager, or tried to join a social group of which the manager was a member, then the manager might treat the speaker with some contempt.

TASK 14

The meanings of the different sentences are:

1 Although someone else might wear the hat, you are not going to be allowed to wear it.

2 You are being emphatically prohibited from wearing the hat by someone in authority.

3 Someone is expressing surprise or even shock that you should consider wearing the hat.

4 Someone is expressing surprise that you are going to wear the hat, but there is also a suggestion that you have made the wrong choice from a range of possibilities.

TASK 15

There is no suggested solution to Task 15.

TASK 16

Photograph (a): A full-time writer, intelligent, with a keen sense of humour. Lives alone. He has an educated Birmingham accent.

Photograph (b): An accountant, lives alone, leads a regulated, ordered life. He has a pronounced Manchester accent.

Photograph (c): An executive secretary, works abroad, single, widely travelled. She is generous and has a good sense of humour. She is from the north of England.

Photograph (d): Successful businessman, interesting and extrovert.

Unless you think in a very unusual way, or your experience of life is vastly different from that of the majority of people, you will notice that you have hit on many of the true facts about the people in the photographs. What this tells us is, that there is a large number of shared preconceptions in any society, which are reinforced by the evidence from real life, showing us how right we were to have them in the first place.

TASK 17

You may well have suggested some of the following reasons.

- The subject matter of what was said was too technical/obscure;
- The explanation was too complicated.
- You presupposed some prior knowledge that the listener did not have.
- You used vocabulary which was unfamiliar to the listener.
- You were thinking about something else or were otherwise distracted, and your explanation lost its logical thread and became confused.

TASK 18

- Sometimes we just fail to recognize the meanings of familiar words because we are not paying enough attention to what is being said.
- Our concentration is allowed to lapse part of the way through what is being said.
- Sometimes we fail to comprehend the importance of several pieces of information when they are put together to show a common thread.
- Thinking about other important issues at the same time as someone is trying to talk to us affects our concentration.
- Much of the vocabulary was unfamiliar to you.

TASK 19

Jennifer might want to know quite a few things about her boss's instructions to her.

1 If Jennifer has not taken the minutes down herself, in her own shorthand, how is she going to have them typed up? Other people's shorthand may be too difficult to understand and transcribe.

2 Assuming that the minutes could be transcribed, she might want to know if her boss wanted to read them for approval before she sent them out.

3 Are the directors' addresses easily available?

4 Does she know what the 'good quality paper and the good-looking envelopes' are?

TASK 20

1 She might ask, 'Mr. Johnstone, were the minutes of the last board meeting taken down in shorthand?' Then she might ask, 'What system of shorthand did the previous secretary use?' If a draft copy has already been prepared, she

might ask, 'Have you checked the draft copy, and is it good enough to be typed up as it is, or are there any alterations you want to make first?'

2 This point has been dealt with above.

3 A simple question like, 'Where is the up-to-date list of directors' addresses kept?'

4 If there is only one lot of good quality paper, then there is no problem, but there may be more than one, so, she should say, 'There seems to be more than one kind of good quality paper, which one should I use? The same applies to the envelopes, which ones do you mean me to use?'

TASK 21

- If Mr Johnstone had gone away on business, Jennifer might have been left with a set of shorthand notes that she could not have transcribed.

- She might have sent the minutes out to the directors in an unacceptable form, or including mistakes, or with important discussion missed out.

- She might have used an out-of-date list of directors, thus sending the confidential minutes to the wrong people. Alternatively, they could have been sent to an old address and still got into the wrong hands.

- Using the wrong quality paper would not be the end of the world, but it shows a lack of care to detail when there is inconsistency. If she were to use poor quality paper and envelopes, some people would feel that it reflected badly on the organization by giving the wrong impression.

TASK 22

a **Key words**: Robinson's of Chester, emergency audit. Someone . . . there now. drop . . . doing . . . Wendy . . . finish . . . go . . . today. Church Street . . . accident. Start . . . purchase ledger . . . attention . . . capital items . . . don't think . . . expenses . . . correct . . . check.

Hearing those words alone would be enough to get the gist of the message Mr Jones wanted to pass on. You may have a different set of words, and it would be useful if you left them aside for a while, then went back and looked at them again before deciding if your 'key words' are the ones which would give you the meaning of what Mr Jones said.

b The sentence which was drowned out by a loud noise, was '. . . because some of those items seem to have been purchased at an inflated figure.'

c The common theme that runs through the passage is the suspicion that not everything that is going on at Robinson's is quite legal.

TASK 23

There is no suggested solution to Task 23.

TASK 24

There is no absolutely right answer to this dilemma, but you ought to have thought of the following:

- You could leave a message for the person you want to speak to, but he/she might not want to speak to you, so they might not return your call.
- If you ask for a time when the person you want to speak to is likely to be there, make a note of it and make sure you call back at that time. Make a note of the person who gave you the information.
- You could ask to speak to someone else who might be able to help.

TASK 25

There is no suggested solution to Task 25.

TASK 26

There is no suggested solution to Task 26

TASK 27

Situation 1. If Mr Grossman's instructions are very strict, then you have to carry them out. You have to stand your ground and say something like:

'I'm sorry but Mr Grossman cannot be reached at the moment, and his secretary is engaged. May I take a message, or get him to call you back?'

If the caller still insists on speaking to Mr Grossman, and the secretary is still engaged, then contact a senior manager and ask him/her to deal with the caller.

Situation 2. Offer to get them a local taxi. Find out their exact location, name and telephone number of current location, and call the taxi for them. If they are only a few minutes walk away, then give them clear, precise directions on how to find you.

Situation 3. Important customers have to be looked after so, it would be better if you could send a car to pick him/her up and bring him/her back to the company's premises. At the same time, arrange for the customer's motoring organization to attend to the car, or get a local garage to do it. Find out from the customer what his organization's arrangements are for such emergencies.

Situation 4. Telling tales on colleagues can be dangerous. Your best course of action would be to tell your colleague that you will pass his message on and leave it at that. After all, he may have a perfectly valid reason for having been on the train. Any problems with his attendance or sick leave record should be identified by his line manager.

Situation 5. You should find out from dispatch if the order is ready to be sent out. If it is, then phone the company you use as a freight forwarder and tell them what your customer wants. Make a note of the details of the flight, its time of arrival in Nairobi, and telephone your customer with them. Apologize to him for the inconvenience and assure him that you will do everything possible to make sure his demands are met. The full number you would dial is 010 254 2 61245. (The form of this number is correct at the time of going to press, but changes in both national and international codes are due in April 1995.)

Situation 6. You should ask your manager if she wants to go first or second class, smoking or non-smoking, what time she wants to arrive in Norwich, and what kind of accommodation she wants in the hotel.

a With regard to your travel agent, you would ask for the class of tickets you wish, with reserved seats, or not, smoking or non-smoking, on a train that would get you to Norwich at the desired time. You would ask him/her to send the tickets to the office, or you might want to collect them.

b As for the hotel, you would book, say, two single rooms with bath or shower, breakfast, and any dietary instructions. The hotel might ask you to send a facsimile as confirmation of your booking.

Telephone Message

Time received:

Name of caller :

Telephone number:

Message:

Date:

From: (their organization)

Received by:

Fig. 13 A telephone message pad

TASK 28

The message pad should be as simple as possible, but should have spaces for certain basic information to be noted:

- The full name of the caller, and his/her organization.
- The time and date of the call.
- The caller's telephone number, even if they say that the person they are calling knows it.
- A brief message including whether or not they wish to be called back.

There are a great many variations on the above which could be adopted for the particular situation you are in, but a sample message pad is shown in Fig. 13 for you to use or adapt as you find necessary.

TASK 29

- The telephone message should have had a date and time on it.
- The nature and time of the Friday meeting should have appeared on it too.
- Mr Andrews' organization and telephone number should have been included.

Step 1. Consult your desk diary to see if any arrangements have been made to see or meet Mr Andrews on a Friday in the near future.

Step 2. See if there is anyone of that name in your list of telephone numbers in the Reading area, and, if there is, call them to see if they have called you that day.

Step 3. Contact anyone else with whom you have a meeting on Friday next to see if they will be accompanied by someone called Andrews.

Step 4. Let Sylvia Conway at the agency know what has happened, so she can show Angela how to avoid such mistakes in the future.

Chapter 2

TASK 30

NOUNS	PROPER NOUNS	COLLECTIVE NOUNS
office	Janice	bunch
desk	Monday	
vase		
flowers		

TASK 31

PRONOUNS:	it (× 2), nobody's, one, It
PERSONAL PRONOUNS:	He, he (× 6)
INTERROGATIVE PRONOUNS:	who
DEMONSTRATIVE PRONOUNS:	That
REFLEXIVE PRONOUNS:	himself
RELATIVE PRONOUNS:	what, which

TASK 32

Sounding good

kind; wonderful; beautiful; enormous; colourful; interesting.

Sounding unpleasant

vicious; spiteful; delapidated; overgrown; dead; unkempt.

TASK 33

Approach Manchester on the M56 continuing to the end of it until it becomes the A5106, and when you get to the first set of traffic lights, remembering to ignore the pedestrian ones, turn right into Barlow Moor road where you will be going in the direction of Didsbury. Go past a filling station on your left until you reach another set of traffic lights where you should turn right and first left on that road. Follow that road until you see another set of lights, where you will see the entrance to our block of flats just before them.

TASK 34

'I work at Johnson's' (SIMPLE PRESENT) – means that Johnson's is my place of work and I go there regularly. 'I am working on my motorbike' (CONTINUOUS PRESENT) – means that I am working on it at the moment. But the difference in meaning between the two forms of the present tense is not quite as simple as that. The continuous present can also be used to express the sense 'at the present time' which could cover a longish period of time, but the difference is that the motor-bike is one single project.

Compare 'I am working on my motorbike' with 'I work on motorbikes'.

'I am renovating an old house' – does not mean that you are doing so at this moment, but it is something you might do in the evenings or at weekends at the present time, but not regularly over a long period of time and it also means that it refers to one project, whereas 'I renovate old houses' refers to a regular activity over a long period of time (long in fact or expectation) involving more than one house.

'We watch television' – means that we watch television on a regular basis. This could be stated with more precision as in:

Every evening we watch the ten o'clock news on television.

'We are watching television' – on the other hand, means watching television now.

'He gets colds in winter' means that he gets colds as a regular occurrence in winter. However, 'He is getting a cold' means that a cold is in the process of developing in him.

TASK 35

The reason for the strange meanings is because the participial constructions are misrelated to the nouns which immediately follow them. You might have spotted:

1 In this sentence, the suit was running from the car.
2 The hole had been digging in the field all day.
3 It looks as if the enemy had been waving the flag.
4 It looks as if the commission had landed the order.

Now look at how you might have rewritten the sentences:

1 Running from his car, the man got his suit soaking wet.
2 Having dug in the field all day, the gang found that the hole collected a lot of water.
3 Waving a flag from the hilltop, the soldier made the enemy advance by mistake.
4 Having landed a big order, the saleman's commission was enormous.

TASK 36

a In 1. it is Arthur; in 2. it is 'the blazing aircraft'; in 3. it is 'the weary traveller'.
b In 1. it is 'tried to find'; in 2. it is 'was abandoned'; in 3. it is 'crawled'.
c In 1. it is 'a job'; in 2. it is 'the injured pilot'; in 3. it is 'a dry barn'.

TASK 37

boats; bays; cargoes; fish (stays the same); they were; quaysides; crews were; inns; some sailors (or sailors, as it is not necessary to make the indefinite article (a) into a plural); were; men; towns.

TASK 38

(1) accumulate; (2) communicate; (3) diverse; (4) malodorous;

(5) precluded; (6) professed; (7) subvert.

TASK 39

collagen – NOUN *French and Greek*

depolitic/ize or -/ise – VERB TRANSITIVE – *nil*

gripe – VERB and NOUN – *Old English, Old High German and West Germanic*

nemesis – NOUN – *Latin*

sally – NOUN and VERB INTRANSITIVE – *French and Old French*

TASK 40

The day the sun disappeared!

Can you imagine anything as frightening as having to live without the sun? Well, that was precisely what happened to a small community on a small Pacific isle one hundred and fifty years ago this week, when Jaime Martinez and his family had been living on the island for about ten years and all their children had been born there.

Jaime and his wife Conchita had moved there with the help of a wealthier brother in order to escape religious retribution. All that time they had enjoyed a good, but simple, life in what had seemed to them Heaven on Earth. But, in the words of the old proverb, 'all good things come to an end'.

On what had dawned as another perfect day on their little farm on this idyllic island Jaime, Conchita and the rest of the two hundred souls believed that they had been visited on by Divine retribution. About eleven o'clock in the morning, the sky became increasingly dark until it was darker than any night, because there was no moon to give them even the faintest of light. Both Jaime and his wife had fallen to their knees and cried out, 'God forgive us and save our children!' but to no avail, as the darkness lasted for two hours, although it had seemed to them to have lasted for a lifetime.

When at last it was over, for of course the sun had not disappeared, it had been nothing more than a total eclipse of the sun, everyone was so relieved. The little community decided to invite a priest to come to their island paradise, and to build a little church so that they could show God they still had faith and to ensure that they would be given Heavenly protection in the future.

TASK 41

Memorandum

To: Jim Johnson, Production Planning Assistant
From: J. Smith, Production Planner   (date)

Re: Staff and machine availability for week commencing (date)

Every Friday afternoon starting at about 1.30 p.m. visit the following sections in the works and speak to the supervisors:

Tool room – Arthur Able
Lathe room – Fred Howland
Grinding room – Bill Jarvis
Polishing room – Ken Bell
Drawing office – Wilfred Smith
Engineering stores – Alex Irlam
Steel stockroom – Peter Eaves

Each supervisor/manager should give you an estimate of machine availability for the following week, noting stoppages for breakdowns, planned maintenance or any other reason, together with an estimate of how long the stoppage will last.

On Monday morning your first task of the day should be to visit the same supervisors and ask them how many of their staff have reported for work, but more importantly, what the work load of each one will be for the week, based on the work in hand.

The information should then be put onto a sheet of paper with appropriate columns on it (an example is attached). The sheet should be attached to a memo which summarizes the information on the sheet and it should be passed to Mr John Giles, Production Planning Manager by 10 a.m. every Monday.

J. Smith

Note that it is not always necessary to put your name at the end of a memo, but some organizations insist on it.

TASK 42

Anthony's Travel

LUXURY MINI COACHES FOR ALL OCCASIONS

28 VICTORIA ROAD . RUNCORN . CHESHIRE . WA7 5BH
TELEPHONE . 0928 561 460

Mr J Williams
43 Roman Walk
Palacefields
RUNCORN
Cheshire
WA4 2LU

24 January 199–

Dear Mr Williams

Our ref: LP Coach-67
Weekend trip to Brussels – April 199–

Thank you very much for your enquiry for a 45-seater coach, destination Brussels, for a weekend excursion next April.

Brussels is not a centre normally included in our holiday itineraries, especially for such a short duration. However, on this occasion, we would gladly make an exception.

This trip would be possible for any weekend in April, leaving Runcorn Old Town Centre at 6 pm on Friday and arriving in Brussels, Hotel Minou, Grande Place at 1 pm on Saturday. The sea crossing will be from Harwich to the Hook of Holland.

On the return journey, the coach will depart from Hotel Minou on Monday at 7 pm, arriving in Runcorn at 12 noon on Tuesday.

The cost per person will be £95 including coach and ferry travel, two nights bed and breakfast in Hotel Minou and a sight-seeing trip round Brussels.

We hope this itinerary will be acceptable and look forward to hearing from you in the near future.

Yours sincerely

Les Pritchard

There are a number of ways the letter could have been written which would be equally acceptable, but in all of them, what you must be aware of is to eliminate the use of over familiar language. The use of contractions is one way that familiarity comes across (don't, can't, etc).

You must also be professional and refrain from telling a prospective customer that you can only consider his/her request because times are hard!

Make sure that your use of language is precise. Spell words correctly, e.g. 'favorably' should be 'favourably'. Remember the rules on salutations and endings of letters.

TASK 43

There is no suggested solution to Task 43.

TASK 44

There is no suggested solution to Task 44.

TASK 45

There are three main points in the first paragraph:

1 The eastbound road to Rize is not grand.
2 The town of Yomra has a camp site.
3 The towns and villages look similar.

In the second paragraph, the five main points are:

4 There are few old Turkish houses.
5 People live in partly finished blocks of flats.
6 The roads are unmade.
7 The beaches are beautiful.
8 The sea is unpolluted.

The first paragraph can now be reduced to:

As the road to Rize becomes less than grand, it passes through many similar looking places, but one of them, Yomra, has a camp site.

And the second paragraph can be reduced to:

The people here live in partly finished blocks of flats, and there are few old Turkish houses. The roads are unmade, but the sea is unpolluted and the beaches are beautiful. (56 words)

Chapter 3

TASKS 46–48

There are no suggested solutions to Tasks 46 to 48.

Chapter 4

TASK 49

(a) The letter: The most important part of the letter is the information about the range of vehicles and their facilities, and the types of contract on offer from *Anthony's Travel*.

(b) The histogram: This is easy. As far as the compiler of this histogram is concerned, the only important thing about it is that the relationship between the two variables, tomato type and yield (presumably crop yield) is made obvious. It is achieved by the use of easily identified blocks.

(c) The Bovril advertisement: The most important thing in the advert is the name! It is written in very large letters indeed. It is advertisements like this one which made it such a household name. Note that every time the name is written, the word appears in larger letters than the others in the sentence. The product is linked to a cosy domestic scene, probably middle class by the size of the kitchen! The concern on the face of the housewife/cook suggests that she will not be able to do any cooking unless the Bovril is found. The fact that the children are devouring the jar of Bovril is there to suggest that it is so tasty that children will even risk chastisement in order to eat it.

TASK 50

1   in this case, 'principal purpose';
2   making the best use of resources and making sure there was a surplus of income over outgoings;
3   traditional views of the RAC were an obstacle to his achieving his goal;
4   similarly, embedded practices prevented him from achieving his goal;
5   long established ways of working;
6   a recording and communication system which relied on handwritten and typewritten methods as opposed to electronic ones;

7   regions which were virtually independent from each other;

8   their main purpose was to change the organization;

9   the overall objectives of the RAC;

10   in keeping with;

11   had the responsibility of re-organizing;

12   each part of the RAC was to be equally accessible in all areas of the country.

Index